The Literature of Cinema

ADVISORY EDITOR: **MARTIN S. DWORKIN**
INSTITUTE OF PHILOSOPHY AND POLITICS OF EDUCATION
TEACHER'S COLLEGE, COLUMBIA UNIVERSITY

THE LITERATURE OF CINEMA presents a comprehensive selection from the multitude of writings about cinema, rediscovering materials on its origins, history, theoretical principles and techniques, aesthetics, economics, and effects on societies and individuals. Included are works of inherent, lasting merit and others of primarily historical significance. These provide essential resources for serious study and critical enjoyment of the "magic shadows" that became one of the decisive cultural forces of modern times.

America
at the Movies

Margaret Thorp

ARNO PRESS & THE NEW YORK TIMES

New York • 1970

Reprint Edition 1970 by Arno Press Inc.
Reprinted by permission of Yale University Press
Reprinted from a copy in The New York Public Library
Library of Congress Catalog Card Number: 75-124039
ISBN 0-405-01639-5
ISBN for complete set: 0-405-01600-X
Manufactured in the United States of America

AMERICA AT THE MOVIES

MARGARET FARRAND THORP

NEW HAVEN · YALE UNIVERSITY PRESS · 1939

FOR

ARTHUR *and* ROSEMARY MIZENER

CONTENTS

ILLUSTRATIONS

FOREWORD

I HAVE long supposed that the quickest way to make friends and pleasant casual acquaintances was to go walking with a dachshund. I know now that it is even better to be writing a book about the movies. People who do not like dogs do not want to talk about dogs but people who do not like the movies are always eager to tell you why. Whether they go to the movies or not everybody in the United States, it seems, cherishes questions or opinions or theories on the art of the motion picture and the range of those questions and theories is amazing. There is, apparently, not a phase of American life which the movies do not somewhere touch. That is a reason for this book.

It is only too vividly apparent, though, that the delights of writing a book about the movies exist only in the imperfect tense. To be writing a book about the movies is one thing; to have written a book is quite another. No book about the movies can be very satisfactory to anyone, least of all to its writer.

Every book about the movies must, in the first place, be written too fast. Years of serious study ought to be undertaken before you set pen to paper but while you are thoughtfully contemplating the motion picture of 1938 the motion picture of 1939 turns precipitately into something completely different and unpredicted. Television, a Federal investigation, perfume projection, or a four-dimensional screen—nothing is impossible—may blow matured conclusions to ludicrous atoms. The art whose essence is motion simply will not be still long enough to allow anyone to look at it properly. Every example one selects to make a point is dimmed next week by a better, if it is not refuted. It is melancholy today to read the things the most acute critics of 1929 and 1930 said about sound. To be anywhere nearly up-to-date in discussing the movies one must write rapidly and superficially. There is so much to say that one is obliged to be inadequate. It is probably essential also to be inaccurate since in the history of the motion picture truth and legend are almost inextricably mixed, primary sources are few, and much important information comes only by hearsay.

The excuse one has for writing at all is that there are so many things that ought to be known, so much amusing and important material flickering in ephemeral publications and on the lips of workers in the art that to assemble some of it between covers where it can be found, examined, and corrected, seems to be a kind of public service. For it is perfectly obvious that people want, and need, to know more about the movies, about what the movies are doing to them and what they can do to make the movies nearer to their hearts' desires. It is perfectly obvious that whether or not they are "your best," motion pictures are your most absorbing entertainment.

THE paragraphs that follow are inadequate but they are not inaccurate.

The two people to whom this book is most deeply indebted are Miss Hettie Gray Baker of Twentieth Century-Fox Films and Miss Gladys Percey of the Paramount Studios in Hollywood. They have opened so many doors for me that it is difficult to imagine how I could have gone to work at all if I had not had the good luck to know them. I think that they are aware of my gratitude but I want the pleasure of setting it down again here.

I am indebted also for a variety of courtesies, information, and assistance to the Legal Department of Twentieth Century-Fox Films, the New York Publicity Departments of Metro-Goldwyn-Mayer, Paramount, RKO-Radio, Twentieth Century-Fox, and Warner Brothers; to the National Board of Review, the Cleveland Public Library, the United States Film Service, the Motion Picture Department of the International Federation of Catholic Alumnae, the New York Public Library, the Museum of Modern Art Film Library, the Princeton University Library, and the Motion Picture Producers and Distributors of America, particularly to the New York office. I realize with regret that not all of these people will be satisfied with the use I have made of the information they have been good enough to give me. I have not always been able to agree with the points of view they expressed but I have tried to present them without distortion and I hope that they will believe in the sincerity of my gratitude for all the time and kindness they bestowed on me.

I am obliged to the *Delphian Quarterly* and to *Current History* for permission to reprint portions of Chapter IV which have appeared in their pages.

I wish also to express my gratitude to the Corporation of Yaddo for the opportunity of writing some chapters of this book under practically ideal conditions. And I should like to extend my thanks to the friends and acquaintances who may recognize here and there on these pages some of their unguarded remarks.

M. F. T.

Princeton,
   August, 1939.

I

EIGHTY-FIVE MILLION
A WEEK

THERE are other people who make the
movies besides the artists and technicians in Hollywood. Eighty-five million Americans go to see a picture
every week. That, from one point of view, is why
the movies are so great an art. That, from another
point of view, is precisely why they are not. In
whichever direction justice lies it is undoubtedly
true that no art has ever been so shaped and influenced by its audience as the art of the cinema.

Only very rarely can the making of a picture be
a one-man job. Equipment is elaborate and expensive; expert technical assistance of many kinds is
necessary to the scenarist or the director who
would realize his idea. If a film is to pay the cost
of its production, to say nothing of profits, it is
essential that it should be seen by a very large
number of spectators. That people should want to

see pictures, that the audience should be pleased, is more important to the movies than to any of the other arts. What pleases eighty-five million Americans?

A certain number of movie goers are vocal about the patterns to which they want their pictures to conform. They establish censor boards; they organize pressure groups; they form Better Film Councils and teach Moving Picture Appreciation classes. They know what they want and they keep telling the producers about it. The other section of the eighty-five million, the larger section, express their opinions silently but emphatically at the box office.

The chapters that follow are an attempt to discover some of the effects both these sections of the eighty-five million are having on the movies. What do they ask from their films and how close do they come to getting it? What devices does Hollywood use to persuade them that it is satisfying their desires, to convince them that they are getting what they want? How do the millions affect the movies and how do the movies affect them? How far are their lives altered by the pictures they see? Who, to begin with, are the eighty-five million? Who goes to the movies?

From the industry's point of view the fundamental fact about the eighty-five million weekly movie-goers is that their number is not nearly large enough. For one thing a great many of them are repeaters, people who go to the movies twice a week, three times, even five. Probably not more than forty million in the whole United States really have the movie habit, and we have a population of one hundred and thirty million.

It should be noted [says a recent report from the office of Will Hays, president of the Motion Picture Producers and Distributors of America] that we are far from the saturation point in movie attendance. Ten years ago it was estimated, and probably accurately, that the total motion picture audience was drawn from approximately 25 per cent of our American population. During the closing months of 1937 an experimental poll indicated that there are still twenty-six million persons over twelve years of age who do not go more than five times a year, and there are millions more who cannot be considered regular patrons of the movies.

The industry's problem is to bring that other twenty-six million into the fold without losing any of the eighty-five million. The pearl of great price, then, is the picture that pleases everybody. So far just two pearls have been found: Charlie Chaplin and Walt Disney. The most lofty critics speak with awe of Chaplin's miming while the man on Main Street goes to see a Chaplin picture just as often as he gets the chance. With Disney, whose productions are far more numerous, the unanimity of enthusiasm is even more striking. On Snow

White and Mickey Mouse it is scarcely possible to find a dissenting voice.

"Walter Elias Disney, creator of a new language of art, who has brought the joy of deep laughter to millions and, by touching the heart of humanity without distinction of race, has served as ambassador of international good-will." That is Yale University conferring an honorary M.A. on the occasion of her two hundred thirty-eighth commencement.

"Hats off to Walt Disney. Here is positively the grandest thing ever offered to the public for entertainment. It appeals to every living person from the ages of 2 to 102. After personally viewing this picture [*Snow White*] 16 times, I regretted to see it leave the town." That is the manager of the Oriental Theater, Beaver City, Nebraska.

But with the two gigantic little figures unanimity ends. For the rest the producer must attempt to satisfy his audience in terms of the greatest happiness of the greatest number. The man he cares most greatly to please, the man to whose tastes and prejudices he pays most deferential attention, is the citizen with an income of more than $1,500 a year who lives in a city with a population somewhere above fifty thousand. He, within those wide boundaries, is the movies' average man. From his pockets comes more than half the industry's revenue. It is his feelings of which the movies must be most tender, his fancies and desires they must try hardest to satisfy. "He" is of course the wrong pronoun. It is really that solid average citizen's wife who commands the respectful attention of the industry, just as, in a smaller group, she regulates the best-seller lists of novels. In that invaluable portrait of the average American city, *Middletown in Transition*, the Lynds set squarely in the lap of the average citizen's wife the responsibility for the tone of the majority of American movies. "In the better class houses, adult females predominate heavily in the audiences and, as one producer remarked, 'set the type of picture that will go.'"

What the adult American female chiefly asks of the movies is the opportunity to escape by reverie from an existence which she finds insufficiently interesting. Better ways of enriching her life, society has not yet taught her. She sees the quickest release from a drab, monotonous, unsatisfying environment in dreaming of an existence which is rich, romantic, glamorous. But dreaming, though a pleasant occupation, is not altogether easy. The making of a really good reverie demands considerable effort both of energy and of imagination. How can the American woman who buys her bread sliced and her peas shelled be expected to concoct her own reveries? At the movies she gets them ready-made, put up in neat two-hour cans.

One of the things she wants most is to be appreciated, not just by implication but right out loud. There is social and psychological significance in the fact that 70 per cent of Gary Cooper's fan mail comes from women who write that their husbands do not appreciate them. Their ideal is still the ideal husband of the Victorian era who told his wife at breakfast every morning how much she meant to him, but that husband is not a type which the postwar American man has any interest in emulating. He prefers to conceal his deeper emotions at breakfast, and during the rest of the day as well. His wife, consequently, has to spend her afternoons at the movies.

In the movies a wife finds it quite worth while to get into a new evening frock for a *tête-à-tête* dinner at home because her husband is sure, by dessert time at least, to take her hand across the intimately small and inconvenient table and say, "Darling, you get lovelier every day." When a cinema husband comes home from a business trip he dashes from room to room in the ultra-modern apartment or even up and down stairs if they live in a colonial cottage in Connecticut, frantic if his wife is not on hand to greet him. If she is away for a week-end he makes fabulously expensive long-distance calls without inquiring the toll rate, or boards a transcontinental airplane because he cannot exist any longer without speaking to her. Of course all this is very often the prelude to a murder but it is on the whole rather less humiliating to be murdered than to be taken for granted. And the movie husband continues his devotion even down to old age.

Women liked *Make Way for Tomorow* not just because the elderly couple were so genuinely devoted to each other but because Pa kept talking about his devotion right up to the door of the Old Ladies Home.

Then there is luxury. The adult American female never has quite enough of that. A good marriage of course implies a husband who is a success and success in our commercial civilization is measured largely in terms of money. The adult female goes to the movies as she reads luxury advertising, so that she may be familiar with the ultimate in Fisher bodies and sable coats. But the movies are far more satisfying than the advertisements. They give her an illusion, as she identifies herself with the heroine of the afternoon, that she is enjoying elegances she may never experience in the flesh. She moves with easy grace about a streamlined penthouse, altering by just a touch the position of the stylized alabaster antelope. She lets a cloak slip unheeded from her shoulders to the floor, though the Chinese brocade that fashions it is so priceless that not the most violent real emotion of which she is capable could possibly cause her to forget it for an instant. She serves a faultless dinner without any effort at all, merely mentioning the number of guests expected to her butler or personal maid while, clad in an exquisitely fragile negligee, she glances over the morning mail. The movie heroine never has more than one child and that child never has to be washed or dressed or punished or got ready for school. It is only necessary to bend over her crib now and then and imprint a kiss fragrant with lace and diamonds.

Every phase of life which the adult Middletown female finds dull or wearing in her own home becomes on the screen an easy and exquisite gesture. Beauty, luxury, and love, those are to her the desiderata of life and, being either overworked or overindolent, her idea of bliss is to attain them practically without effort. A not altogether rational ideal but the movies did not impose it on her; they have merely expertly materialized the Platonic shadows of her desires. In the same spirit they provide escape into adventure and excitement for those whose lives are too sedentary or monotonous, and into laughter, which is needed by almost everybody.

After he has pleased the cities of fifty thousand the producer begins to consider the others, also in terms of size, for American taste, apparently, is not sectional but numerical. Only the South seems to be regionally conscious. *They Won't Forget*—which concerned a Southern town's lynching of a schoolteacher suspected of murder chiefly because he was a Northerner—could not be shown in theaters below Washington. Mervyn LeRoy, its director, was, the report goes, surprised. He made *They Won't Forget* because he thought it was a good story; he did not expect the South to take it

Excitement and glamour are what most of the eighty-five million want in their movies. They are demonstrated here by Tyrone Power as Jesse James and by Paulette Goddard.

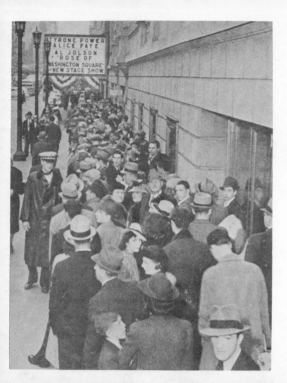

America has seventeen thousand movie theaters. The small town sees, a few weeks later, the same pictures that run on Broadway.

personally. The North, on the other hand, has so forgotten the emotions of the War between the States that a New England audience is no more insulted by the sight of Yankee troops burning a Mississippi mansion (*So Red the Rose, Gone with the Wind*) than by the spectacle of Tartar hordes at the gates of Pekin.

There are seventeen thousand motion picture theaters in the United States, situated in more than nine thousand towns. It is difficult to get out of range of a movie palace anywhere in the country. Even Nevada which, except for Delaware, reckons the smallest number, has forty, while New York, Pennsylvania, and Illinois each counts hers at more than a thousand. It is not surprising to find theaters, big and little, in the cities but there are more than three thousand small towns, numbering their citizens by hundreds, which have moving picture theaters. The twelve million American negroes seem to be the only considerable section of the population who cannot go to a movie whenever they have the price. Some Southern cinemas reserve special sections for negroes. Others do not admit them at all. There are a few negro theaters; about one for every twenty-one thousand negroes.

Among the rest of the population the seat-for-every-twelve people, which is the national average, ranges from a-seat-for-every-eight in New England to a-seat-for-every-twenty-one in the East South Central states. Admission charges run all the

way from $2.20, and even more, for first showings
in big urban theaters to 10¢ in the farm districts
and the third- and fourth-run city houses. The
most usual price is 25¢ or 35¢.

It is in the small town that tastes are most definitely marked. The subtle, the exotic, the unexpected they do not like at all, and they are frankly
annoyed by costume pictures. "Just try to kid the
farmers this is entertainment," writes a despairing
exhibitor after running a Fred Astaire dance film
in Fertile, Minnesota. "We just can't sell costume," says Lincoln, Kansas. "A lavish production
[*Marie Antoinette*] which will please the small
percentage of your patrons who are at all interested
in French history. We could have gotten better
box-office results from almost any program picture
produced at a small fraction of the cost of this
one." That is Manassa, Colorado. "Our audience
does not like costume pictures and when Hollywood gets this into its vast void of skull, we will
all be better satisfied. We no sooner get through
with *Antoinette* than along comes *The Great
Waltz* [Strauss], another headache." Ligonier,
Indiana. Comments like those are found in the interesting department, "What the Picture Did for
Me," run weekly in the *Motion Picture Herald*.

The rural moviegoer likes to feel at ease with
his art. That is one reason why the serial is so
popular. The city dweller who swallows a different brand of art every evening is practically ob-

livious to the delights of living on from week to
week with the same set of characters, people whom
you've known for a long time but find much more
interesting than most of your actual friends. You
can have your weekly artistic experience, if you
are a serial fan, without the labor of adjusting
yourself each time to a wholly new environment.
The devotee of the "Lone Ranger" watches his
tenth adventure with the same comfortable ease
with which the experienced musician hears a new
conductor's reading of Beethoven's "Seventh Symphony." Serials therefore are many and their range
is wide. New serials are being started every year.
There are the domestic comedies in which the fans
see the children grow and change naturally like
the children in their own households. Just as far
as possible the movie companies keep the same
players in the same parts. There are the thrillers,
the girl reporter "Torchy Blaine," the "Mysterious
Pilot," the "Spider," the "Saint," "Bulldog Drum-
mond," "Charlie Chan." And there are the peren-
nial Westerns with special heroes like Gene Autry
(Public Cowboy No. 1), Bill Boyd, Buck Jones,
and Dick Foran. A good many serials are based
on syndicated newspaper strips which gives them
a double familiarity. "Flash Gordon," "Buck
Rogers," "Dick Tracy," "Blondie," "Little Orphan
Annie." The wise small-town operator knows just
which ones his patrons want most.

Because of this liking for the flavor of familiarity

imported pictures do not have a very wide circulation in America. One hundred and seventy-five theaters in eighty-five communities ran foreign language films in 1939 and half of those did not show them exclusively. Once or twice a year a much publicized picture, like *Grand Illusion* which the critics voted the best foreign film of the year, will play the larger theater circuits but in general even the English-speaking foreign actors whom Hollywood likes to import are not popular. They wear their glamour with a difference which the cities find piquant and charming but which is only annoying to the provinces. "They may have gone nuts over *Tovarich* [played by Charles Boyer and Claudette Colbert] in Paris, London, and New York, but the audience displayed no such enthusiasm here in Indiana. It laid an egg, as we expected it to do." There are complaints about the "dialect" which the 100 per cent American must make a heavy effort to understand. "Annabella will be O.K. after she learns to speak English." "Luise Rainer is a wonderful artist but she is not popular here. Think because she is hard to understand." Or, *To the Victor* (made from the famous dog story *Bob, Son of Battle*) is a "well produced picture but not for American audiences. Unfortunately we did not have the foresight to engage an interpreter to explain the meaning of the Scotch dialect. The only word we understood was 'Aye,' of which there was enough to float a presidential election. I do not recommend this for small-town theaters." That tirade is from upstate New York. "We dust-bowl dwellers," comes another wail, "do not appreciate English conversation." In Indiana they object even to the Bryn Mawr patois of Katharine Hepburn.

When he wants glamour the farmer wants it thick and obvious. The ideal seems to be Dorothy Lamour. "A commentator on a near-by large-town paper," writes a small-town manager in Texas, "rated *Her Jungle Love* as pure hokum. If that is the case let's have lots more hokum; this drew a capacity house here." "A small-town natural if there ever was one," writes another. "People in Cedartown go for Dorothy Lamour in a big way." "My rural patrons enjoyed this."

Even more than glamour the farmer and the small-town man want excitement. A good mystery or intrigue film can keep a whole village talking for days. The current movie plot takes the place of local gossip. The woman who went last night rings up her friend on the telephone to retail every item of the story. She goes over each significant gesture and movement of the heroine with the same loving care she would lavish on the activities of a giddy neighbor. And art is as usual more satisfactory than life. The neighbor may turn out to have been engaged in some perfectly ordinary and exemplary occupation. In the movies there really is an intrigue or a murder, a missing heir or a po-

tential triangle. Besides it is possible to know all
the interesting details, to see what goes on in the
parlor even if the blinds are down. Those emotions
which the small town used to purge by gossip now
have a wider channel in the cinema.

Even better than the excitement of intrigue the
small town likes the obvious excitement of Westerns, the hard riding and the gun play. They were
badly disappointed in Farmerville, Louisiana, when
they found that *Conquest* was just a story about
Napoleon and a lady and had no shooting in it
at all. Lemmon, South Dakota, simply walked out
on it. Big spectacles with disasters or fights are
popular, *Stagecoach*, *Dodge City*, *Suez*, *Jesse
James*; and the enthusiasts can take their excitement
in even cruder form. *Dracula* and *Frankenstein*
and the other "thrill-shockers" flourish. If an exhibitor can persuade his audience that the picture
is capable of scaring them into hysterics his week
is made. One of the Film Year Books presents,
in a department of advice to theater managers, a
"ballyhoo" which many exhibitors have found
effective:

"Have a nurse in attendance. She works with
a 'plant,' who faints at each performance. The
'casualty' is taken from the theater front in an
ambulance, in full view of the lines waiting to go
in. The plant gets a ride for a few blocks, and
then walks back to do the act over at the next
showing."

The desire to be scared to death is by no means confined to the provinces. When the 1939 revivals were in progress someone had the idea of double-billing *Dracula* and *Frankenstein* and daring the public to see them both in the same evening. From Seattle to Waterbury, Connecticut, the theaters were stormed. In Salt Lake City a crowd of four thousand, impatient to have their blood run cold, broke through police cordons and smashed the windows of the box-office in their eagerness to have the terror begin. A new combination was tried, *Bride of Frankenstein* and *Dracula's Daughter*. The audiences kept on coming.

This socio-economic classification of his audience is far more important to the producer than a division in terms of age. The moviegoing period runs all the way from fourteen to forty-five. The number of younger attendants is not large enough to make the manufacture of special films for their benefit a very profitable business. Whatever you give them they won't pay more than a dime. To the Women's Clubs and Parent-Teacher Associations, who clamor for fairy tales and such wholesome fare, the industry listens listlessly. It would not pay. Besides, children who go to the movies with any degree of regularity become so accustomed to adult pictures that they scorn anything simplified for their benefit in theme or technique. For children's matinées it is always possible to draw a crowd with Westerns, mysteries, or the filmings of very popular stories like *Heidi* and *Tom Sawyer*. On other occasions, let the children go to a "family" picture.

The age distinction in films which England makes by labeling pictures "a"—a small "a"—for adult, America achieves by the more positive and beguiling classification "family." Much in vogue with Better Film Councils and other givers of advice to the public, the designation has been welcomed by the industry. It does not, like "adult," warn the weak away but invites everyone to come in. The family picture is certified to contain no "sophisticated" situation which it might embarrass father to witness by his little daughter's side, and be called upon to explain. *Stablemates* is an example of the ideal family picture. "I would rate this," writes an Oklahoma exhibitor, "as a three handkerchief picture for the ladies. The men will get theirs from the racehorse angle and the kids will fall for Mickey. What more could you ask?"

Within the general outlines of taste the producer is watchful for seasonal variations, trends, whims, changes of public mood. These appear to him to be quite illogical and unpredictable. His attitude towards his public is very like that of the sailor towards the sea. The sailor may guess what the sea is going to do but he can never be sure. So the producer. He becomes in consequence highly superstitious, believing in his luck, trusting to hunches, working by feel. He has a profound belief in the movement of popular taste by cycles but he is skeptical of the possibility of predicting cycles scientifically. It is true that *Over the Hill to the Poorhouse* was a big success in the boom days when people were ready to take their escape by way of a good cry. When the depression came, poorhouses were too close to reality. Audiences wanted to be cheered up when they went to the movies; they had no desire to see on the screen the squalor and misery of which there was all too much at home. Today, when life is a little less immediately uncomfortable yet thick on every hand with threats and horror, the audience likes to get away from its present into the realms of history. But that history must be full of movement and action and color. In this era of aerial bombings and wholesale slaughter we sup so full of horror in every daily newspaper that no ordinary occurrence can touch our nerves at all. Nothing smaller than an earthquake, a hurricane, a fire, or a flood seems to us even interesting. What we need to excite us is "hundreds of people killed in a new and diverting way," as a theater advertisement put it recently.

Such attitudes are worth noting but the producer is wary of pushing sociological explanation too far. Publishers may think in such concepts but they are dealing with a special and a tiny audience. For the producer the biographical cycle in motion pictures is probably not related to the increased reading of

biography; the American history cycle is not a
product of our growing nationalism. People go to
biographical films because they saw *Zola* and liked
it. They enjoyed *The Plainsman* and *In Old Chicago* so they went to see *Marco Polo* and *Robin
Hood*. It is the romance and adventure that count;
the locale is unimportant. The G-man cycle, the
mysteries, the musicals, the goofy comedies, the
films built round opera stars, the stories about
doctors are all to be accounted for by some big
successful picture that, for a reason, probably in-
scrutable, struck the public fancy and set the wheel
spinning. It will not do to rely too much on theories in this gamble of production where you must
work nearly a year ahead of the game. You have
to play your hunches.

In the spring of 1938 the producers had a hunch
that the country was swinging into an action cycle.
Action was the "keynote" of all the spring sales
campaigns; something happening every minute
and whenever possible something happening in
technicolor. Warner Brothers dramatized the
idea at a New York sales convention when they
gathered into the Hotel Roosevelt the men who
were to peddle Warner films to exhibitors over
half the country. The sales manager stood upon
a platform in the ballroom and addressed his forces.
"Boys," he said, "you want action. You've been
praying for action and, by heaven, you're going
to get action." He tapped his gavel gently and the

startled salesmen found themselves gasping in a cloud of smoke and shots. Hidden tommy guns were discharging all over the room. When the confusion had quieted a bit it was explained that the volley had sounded the "keynote" for the season: "Our slogan is going to be, 'Warner Brothers will give you action in 1938.'" In 1939 the hunch was strengthened by theory and the "keynote" was action-plus-Americanism. *The Sea Hawk, Nevada, Spawn of the North, Northwest Passage, The Oklahoma Kid, Stagecoach, Dodge City, Union Pacific;* the titles are all in key.

There is one other division among the eighty-five million which the producer is sometimes forced to make, a division by intelligence. When it can be done without boring the others, who are more important because more numerous, the industry delights to win the approval of the "class" audience, the "intellectuals," as it politely calls them, who want "art" in their movies and "content" as well as escape and excitement and glamour.

The easiest response to their requests is to point out how rich the films are in facts and news, how much anyone can learn by going to the movies. The enormous amount of general information absorbed by the moviegoing child and the painless ease with which it is retained have long been a cause of heart searching to educators. The small-town boy in Vermont or Arkansas who has never in his life been fifty miles from the farm is now

quite at home on the *Place de la Concorde*, Broadway at midnight, the Himalayas, or any one of a
dozen South Sea islands. He knows something
about coal mining, about radio broadcasting, deep
sea fishing, and bridge building, and he has a pretty
good idea of how the United States looked in the
gold rush period and during the Civil War. Every
month, too, he picks up two or three new skills.
He learns in March how to build an igloo, in
April how to train a Siamese elephant, in May
how to cut up a whale—not vocationally useful
perhaps but broadening, just the sort of thing our
best progressive schools teach elaborately by the
project method. And he gets a lot of thoroughly
practical information besides: what sort of hat to
wear with evening clothes, the proper manner
towards a head waiter, how to make an impression
on your girl by your way of delivering wisecracks,
how to buy a ticket for a transcontinental plane;
all these things the pictures will teach him. The
most banal of screen stories may have its educational value as a portrait of life in eighteenth-century Vienna or as a course in ocean-liner etiquette.

Then there is the newsreel. Practically every one
of the seventeen thousand movie theaters shows
two newsreels a week. Two reels are made by each
of the five newsreel companies, Fox Movietone,
News of the Day, Paramount, RKO-Pathé, and
Universal. A good many of the larger theaters
buy several of these and make up a composite

newsreel of their own. It may be true that not all of the typical newsreel can be classified as educational; the sight of the alligator who rides a bicycle, the Queen of the Lima Bean Festival, or the inventor of an amphibious automobile which can be kept in the bathtub may not raise anybody's I.Q. very far, but those are interludes and the American audience, with its admirably lively if undisciplined curiosity, is thoroughly interested in what happened last week in Germany or China, what an invention, deadly or beneficent, looks like, how the ceremony they could not attend was carried out, and how the man of the hour smiles and speaks. Probably because the newsreel is so accepted a part of the staple program the special newsreel theater does not flourish. There are not a dozen of them at present in the country.

The steadily growing popularity of the monthly releases of *The March of Time* is another indication of the desire for information. You have to cultivate, according to exhibitors, a taste for *The March of Time*, but, once cultivated, the taste endures. Patrons even ask their theater manager to let them know whenever a new issue is to be shown. When the series was put on the market in 1935 it appeared in 432 theaters. Today it is released in some eleven thousand. The premise on which the two-reel (twenty-minute) feature is based seems to be sound: current events are more interesting when they are presented in dramatic continuity, even if some of that continuity has to be staged; and people want to know not merely what happened but why. Each issue deals usually with three subjects, one foreign, one national, and one in lighter vein, but each has time to cover its subject far more thoroughly than the ordinary newsreel.

The desire for films that tell you something, the intellectuals seem to share, conveniently, with the rest of the eighty-five million. When they ask from their movies artistic experience the industry is put to a little more trouble. America has never been cordial to the little theater for the selected audience which is the solution that British promoters of the artfilm continually propose for the movies-for-the-intellectual problem. The little theater is not sufficiently remunerative to interest most American magnates. The American method is to lead the intellectuals gently into the general fold by showing them that the movie that pleases the millions may also offer artistic experience as rich as any to be found in book or play or painting. The "prestige pictures" made with conscious, and frequently awkward, gestures towards the intellectuals are usually less successful in proving the point than the steadily improving technique of the less pretentious film. The eighty-five million have not the least objection to beautiful camera work, first-class acting, or high directoral skill if it does not dim their reveries or slow down their adven-

Only two makers of movies succeed in pleasing everybody: Charles Chaplin, whose films (this is "Modern Times") combine comedy and satire; and Walt Disney, whose cartoon creatures have become part of America's folklore.

The future of the film may lie in the movie which interests different audiences at different levels. To subtle directing and acting "Love Affair" adds romance, sentiment, and glamour.

Some audiences saw "They Won't Forget" as a social document, others as cinema art, others as a murder mystery.

tures. The movie seems to be quite as capable of proceeding on two levels as the Elizabethan tragedy: poetry and psychology for the gentlemen's galleries, action and blood for the pit. The screen has not yet developed its Shakespeare but the varying responses which even now one sees made to the same film are surely not without significance. A theater manager, for instance, in Penacook, New Hampshire, reports that Pare Lorentz's *The River* is "best appreciated by your class trade but will not disappoint the average." Imaginative and experimental, *The River* was made for the United States Government to show how we took the Mississippi valley apart by frenzied cotton cultivation and reckless deforesting and how we have the power to put it together again. "We booked this," writes a state prison director of recreation about *The Good Earth*, "to satisfy the more intelligent group but it seemed to please all." "Was afraid of this for my small town," says a Wisconsin exhibitor of *The Life of Emile Zola*, "didn't need to be, as I found that even the lower classes enjoyed it." Mervyn LeRoy's *They Won't Forget* was received by critics as an extraordinarily skillful piece of cinema technique. Those who consider thinking entertainment (with the exception, as we have seen, of the South) found it a courageous treatment of lynch law and sectional prejudice. An exhibitor in a small town in the State of Washington reports: "One of the surprise pictures of the year. Folks are still trying to figure out who killed the girl." The Cozy Theater, Cabool, Missouri, thought it "an entertaining picture that packs a terrific wallop," and reports, "Did about average business and heard no complaints, although several people wanted to know who the actual murderer was." *Young Mr. Lincoln*, skillfully directed by John Ford and beautifully acted by Henry Fonda, pleased both the aesthetes and those interested in pictures with ideas. After running it in Connellsville, Pennsylvania, a theater manager writes: "Business better than average," and from Dewey, Oklahoma, comes the report: "Good picture and good business. No complaints but many compliments." Dewey also says of *Juarez*, whose beauty of photography and dignified handling of a serious theme caused the Congress of American writers to vote it the best screen play of the year: "A very good picture which did above average business. Being a historical drama I did not expect much business in this small town but was pleasantly surprised." Old Town, Maine, thought it "big enough for extended runs in all spots."

Although not all the small-town and rural patrons agree in their enthusiasm for pictures of this kind these different levels of criticism—approval of the same picture for often quite different reasons —deserve far more study than anyone has yet given them. In the picture on two levels may lie the whole solution of the problem of movies for the million.

Here, then, is an outline portrait of the eighty-five million who make the movies by putting down their quarters at the box-office. The succeeding chapters examine in more detail some of their desires, expressed and implied, what they go to the movies to find, how far they are getting it, and some of the things they get in addition to those for which they pay their weekly quarters.

II

WHAT MOVIE TONIGHT?

———————————————————————

WHEN any one of the eighty-five million moviegoers walks down Main Street of an evening saying, "Shall we go to the Majestic or the Bijou?" he imagines that he is making up his mind about his evening's entertainment. As a matter of fact the nightly decision is very far from being a matter of free will. The choice was predestined months ago, predestined by forces working so steadily and so subtly that the chooser is usually quite unaware how he got it fixed in his mind that *The Life of Mr. Blank* is a film he really ought to see. For the last six months or more that idea has been impinging upon him constantly, painlessly, obliquely, without his really being aware of its presence until the moment for action came.

The pressure began when the Vice President in Charge of Sales, or whatever he happens to be called, sat in at a conference in Hollywood to plan

the schedule for the season. It was his job to pass not
on the artistic or narrative beauties of the stories
brought up for consideration but upon their exploitation qualities. His farsighted eye marked the
"tie-up" between *Robin Hood* and the schools,
between *Wells Fargo* and the express companies,
between *You're a Sweetheart* and the local caterer.
He thought, too, about the sales value of titles. He
was likely to urge the desirability of filming a well-
known comic strip, a popular novel, or a Pulitzer
Prize play for on those titles some tens of thousands
of dollars' worth of advertising has been already
done. With them it is possible to reckon, too, on
that widespread human eagerness to experience the
same story in as many media as possible. If you've
read the book you must see the play. If you saw
the play you want to see the film. It seems to be
part of the desire for familiarity in a strange world
which attracts people to serials. Man wants to get
out of his own setting but not to feel a complete
stranger in the new one. If he can place some of
the landmarks in his new environment or recognize one or two of the passers-by he experiences
an agreeable sensation of adjustment and superiority, the sensation one gets from speaking the language adequately in a foreign country. Fortunately
the thing works both ways and the people who
hadn't the patience to read a much publicized novel
feel guilty and go to see the film.

As soon as the pictures have been decided upon

the sales manager begins to plan his season's campaign, gathering his forces into sectional and national conventions, sounding the keynote of the year, revealing to them what wonder has been designed for Christmas holiday release and what for Easter. The salesmen set out to spread the good news, and the films, among the theaters. When they can offer with a picture the producer's promise to back it with a heavy advertising campaign they have something as useful as the assurance that it will be played by top box-office stars.

National advertising campaigns have their routine procedure, and their special features if the picture is big enough. The companies design billboard, magazine, and newspaper advertising, make press books of suggestions to theater men, and plan material for lobby displays. Some of the posters, "stills," "blowups," and "cutouts" for local use must be rented by the theater but the company makes them. Their quantity and quality vary with the importance of the picture. On a feature film specially dear to his heart a producer will announce his intention to run full color pages in a half-dozen magazines with national circulation, or promise to double his usual advertising, or agree to spend at least $100,000. He will print elaborate maps showing his nationwide billboard campaign. All this is dreamed and executed while the picture is in production. A feature campaign may get under way even before the cameras turn.

One successful device is that Selznick specialty, the hunt for talent. The film the producer finds difficulty in casting must be based of course on a very well-known book or play. Audiences must be already panting to see some beloved character on the screen. That the perfect actor may be found for the role the producer turns for advice to the fans. That device was used for *Gone with the Wind*. Fans love to write letters. The producer will get all the suggestions he can assimilate. He may even have to adopt some of them. Newspapers and magazines will help him, too, by balloting their readers. Everybody will help him by discussing his problem. *Gone with the Wind* was a national, and international, question for two and a half years.

The other method is to ride up and down the countryside looking for the perfect type. Somewhere in the United States, Selznick argued, there must be a twelve-year-old boy with freckles, curly hair, and the grin of the ideal *Tom Sawyer*. For nine months talent scouts went abroad in the land. They looked, by actual count, at 25,000 children; they gave screen tests to 500. They tried the obvious sources of supply: theatrical schools, the children of actors, the thousands of boys whose fond parents presented them in response to radio broadcasts and newspaper appeals. They visited beaches along the California coast. They went to orphan homes. They went to parks and playgrounds. They got two thousand Boy Scouts to march to the Gilmore Stadium for inspection. They enlisted the help of English teachers in the Chicago public schools and the teachers in all the schools, public, private, and parochial, in St. Louis. At last they found him, as might have been expected, by chance. He was playing on the street near his home in the Bronx, with no thought of the movies in his head.

A good deal can be done for "build-up" while the picture is in production. The weight of some films is carried entirely by their stars; others must pull their own or at least help. Some films are rich in production stories. Sometimes it is a setting, sometimes a scene or property. In Norma Shearer's *Marie Antoinette*, for instance, it was Versailles. Louis' *Galerie des Glaces* wasn't large enough; they had to build a bigger and better palace.

In *Romance in the Dark* the lovely Gladys Swarthout was required to let herself be struck in the eye by a tomato. That tomato swelled to a size which astonished even Paramount's publicity department. It grew to international proportions. Newspapers talked of it on two continents. Hot letters were written about it. Chambers of Commerce kept shipping in tomatoes. The selection was made with care and California was chagrined when the choice fell upon a tomato from Florida. Reporters and photographers flocked to the studio for the shooting of the scene. A piece of steak was

In a drive-in theater you watch the show from your own automobile.
This one is in Burbank, California. There are about a dozen in the
United States.
Silver Theater, Silver Spring, Maryland. In his local movie theater
many an American first encounters modern architecture.

The exploitation of motion pictures is a new American art. "Stagecoach" inspired this lobby display at Loew's Poli in New Haven. A "tie-up" with nature arranged by the manager of the Palace Theater, Gary, Indiana.

thirty-five hundred, the proceeds going to the Red Cross.

For *Marie Antoinette* "Marionette Moviettes" were invented and sent on a two-year tour of the United States and Europe. Thirty-inch tall marionettes play, behind glass, scenes from the picture, their actions synchronized to sound track records of voices of the performers. The success was so great that "moviettes" are being made of other important productions.

Robin Hood, which seems for many reasons destined to become a landmark in movie history, was hailed by the trade journals as an exploitation man's dream. The press book which Paramount issued for the guidance of theater men ran to sixty pages and contained, among other riches, "one hundred exploitation ideas" and "twenty-five national tie-ups and promotions." Perhaps the only people not perfectly pleased with the *Robin Hood* exploitation were the nation's parents whose offspring spent weeks in shooting chickens, cats, and each other with bows and arrows. The opening shot of that great national flight was fired at an elaborately planned tournament in Palm Springs just as the picture went into circulation.

As the date of a picture's showing approaches exhibitors find the trailer one of their most effective instruments. It is so effective that the making of trailers has become almost a separate art. Trailers

seem to have got their name from the little advertising pictures that trailed on after the feature in
some of the smaller theaters. They are now coming
to be spoken of as "previews of coming attractions." Various companies have engaged in the
business of making them since they first began to
be used in 1920, but with the development of
sound their production became more expensive and
now most of the manufacturing for the country is
in the hands of the National Screen Corporation.
Recently Warner Brothers and then MGM began
to make their own trailers, a practice very likely
to spread. Not only have the companies all the
necessary mechanical equipment to hand but the
stars as well, and that is important in the modern
theory of trailer making. It does not do, it is now
believed, just to clip scenes from the film or to
utilize strips taken by the extra cameras. It is better
to turn the trailer itself into a little skit in which
the stars clown or sing or talk about the show and
give the previewer some conception of the kind
of picture he will see if he comes next week. The
idea is that if a spectator is amused by a trailer he
will be more likely to think kindly of the coming
attraction. When the film itself is rather weak in
audience appeal a heavy strain is imposed upon the
integrity of the trailer maker. He is forbidden to
show anything that spoils the picture's story or
gives away the climax but he is tempted to pick
out a lurid bit of action, even if it is not typical,

or risk a shot that would never be allowed in the completed film. The censors, therefore, insist on including trailers in their examinations. Sometimes the subterfuges resorted to by trailer makers are comparatively harmless, like the advertising of *Generals without Buttons* by stills and English captions so as not to frighten away an English-speaking audience. Just so it could feel that it had been truthful, the trailer faded out to boys' voices singing a French song.

When the film is completed the picking of a strategic spot for a world première (pronounce it preméer) is an important move in every big exploitation campaign. Sometimes the places of opening is clearly indicated. It was obvious to anyone that *The Buccaneer* must open in New Orleans; *The Texan* in San Antonio; *Man of Conquest*, i.e., Sam Houston, in Houston; that *Rawhide*, with Lou Gehrig, should see the light in Saint Petersburg where the Yankees were training; *Sons of the Legion*, at the Los Angeles convention; and the crooning, horse racing *Sing, You Sinners*, at Saratoga in August.

Sometimes ingenuity must be utilized to find the desired city. *Of Human Hearts* opened in Greenville, South Carolina, because that was the home of the young man who won the $5,000 prize in the contest that named the picture. Metro-Goldwyn-Mayer opened *Servant of the People*, the first of a series of historical shorts, in the guardroom of old Fort Wood which is built into the base of the Statue of Liberty. Paramount showed *Spawn of the North* in Blowing Rock, North Carolina, to an audience of one hundred and sixty-two Blue Ridge mountaineers, each of whom signed an affidavit that he had never seen a movie before. *Gunga Din* was so supercolossal that it got a triple première, New York, Miami, and Hollywood all on the same night. *Dodge City* Warner's opened in Dodge City—population now about ten thousand —sending from Hollywood to Kansas a special train bearing stars, columnists, radio commentators, two newsreels crews, and a complete broadcasting studio. They were welcomed by the Governors of Kansas, Colorado, and New Mexico and by Dodge City potentates who carried horse pistols and had grown whiskers in honor of the occasion. The entertainment included street dancing, a rodeo, and forty-five bands.

The resulting publicity was such that it became the fashion for producers to "take Hollywood to the nation." For *Union Pacific* Paramount staged in Omaha "the biggest costume party America has ever had," with ten thousand citizens in the dress of 1860, Main Street shop fronts remodeled to suggest the old West, and a tribe of Sioux camped on the Courthouse lawn. After "Golden Spike Days" had come to a climax with the première of the film, the "Union Pacific Special Train" bore its Hollywood notables east, stopping for openings of the picture in forty-five different cities.

Twentieth Century-Fox added government officials, educators, and historians to the Hollywood lights it transported to Springfield, Illinois, for the première of *Young Mr. Lincoln* at which Marian Anderson sang, broadcasting over a national network.

Occasionally, of course, there is a fiasco, like the one in Columbus City, Indiana, selected for the world première of *White Banners* because it was the birthplace of the author, Lloyd Douglas. A thriving little place of thirty-eight hundred, Columbus City took offense at what appeared to be an attempt to present it as the hick town that had cradled a famous writer. The citizens stayed rather conspicuously away from the parade of welcome and Douglas' speechmaking, and left the house half empty at the première. They waited to see the picture on the second night when the price of tickets dropped back from seventy-five cents to the usual thirty.

But Columbus City is the exception; the exploitation man does not often go wrong. He is practiced in making geography work for him, nature too, and any national or international event that can be counted upon to run off on schedule. *Snow White* was released during the Christmas holidays; *Touchdown, Army* in October; *Having*

Wonderful Time at the peak of the summer vacation season. *Tom Sawyer's* opening coincided with Children's Book Week. *The Prince and the Pauper* consoled those Americans who could not go to England for the coronation.

More impressive though more conventional than the special opening is the Hollywood première. The cost is enormous but the results in newspaper space and pictures seem to justify the cost. All the stars from the other companies who have to go help advertise the new picture as do all the other celebrities in a town which holds at any given time more world recognized names than any other city on the globe. Canny men like Samuel Goldwyn make very sure that no news photograph of any glamorous star from another lot can be run without a mention of the première she was attending. When he opened *The Hurricane* Goldwyn had hung about the neck of each member of the audience a *lei.* This cost a thousand dollars but that is negligible in an expense account mounting to thirty or forty thousand. The searchlights and spots, without which Hollywood would not believe in the opening of even a filling station, come to some three thousand dollars. Bleachers have to be built for hundreds of onlookers, and insured in case they should collapse. A public address system must be installed and a radio hookup arranged. Elaborate souvenir programs must be printed. The largest expense of all is usually the advertising. Some spectacular device has to be invented in order to convince a town living continually on the top plane of the superlative that this is an event of really huge proportions, one that simply must not be missed.

After the première comes the road showing or the Broadway opening or the first run. It depends on the degree of prestige desired. The roadshow is really a relic of the day when the movie was trying to prove itself as good as the theater, to get itself taken seriously. The important picture moves majestically through a line of key cities—usually New York, Chicago, Philadelphia, Boston, Los Angeles, San Francisco—accompanied sometimes by special musicians or other acolytes, always by a group of publicity men. The showings take place in the best houses. There are only two performances a day, matinée and evening, and the price is a theater price, $2.20. In the early days this was a guarantee of high art. Now the distinction is becoming a little blurred; the patrons are aware that prices will go down in a week or two. There were ten road shows in 1937. The plans for the next season eliminate them almost entirely though some producers still contend that road showing is the best way to impress the masses with a class picture.

The Broadway opening is more likely to make money and it does make an impression on the trade. It helps in selling the picture to exhibitors in the

provinces. At least it did. There is an increasing
feeling among managers sensitive to their communities that Broadway is not precisely the measure of national taste. What goes there, as we have
seen, will not necessarily go in Cedartown and
Mechanicsville.

Then there are special screenings. Before a film
is released to the greedy public it is often worth
while to call it to the attention of some particular
group. People will come by invitation to a special
showing of a picture concerning their profession
who would walk past the theater lights seven times
without a glance, and people who are invited to a
preview talk about it to their friends. The secretary of a medical association asked to a special
screening of *Pasteur* will voluntarily send out letters to all the members of his organization telling
them that here at last is a moving picture that takes
science seriously. The Rotary Club will say a good
word for the lesson of *The Boss Didn't Say Good
Morning;* the Boy Scouts for *Lord Jeff* or *The
Plainsman.* Express company officials who pre-
viewed *Wells Fargo* certified its authenticity by
posters on all their wagons. A thousand members
of the Life Underwriters Association of New York
City opened National Insurance Week by seeing
Make Way for Tomorrow, and announced that
"without being propaganda the picture constitutes
about the finest plea for old-age security that has
ever been presented to the American public. Every

life insurance agent in the country ought to see this film."

But the movies are not content to rely on the advertising of their loving friends. They like to talk about themselves. From its earliest days movie advertising has shrilled superlatives. There is a eulogy of the art written in 1896 by one of Edison's laboratory assistants which sets the key. The motion picture, it begins, is

the crown and flower of nineteenth century magic, the crystallization of Eons of groping enchantments. In its wholesome, sunny and accessible laws are possibilities undreamt of by the occult lore of the East, the conservative wisdom of Egypt, the jealous erudition of Babylon, the guarded mysteries of Delphic and Eleusinian shrines. It is the earnest of the coming age, when the great potentialities of life shall no longer be in the keeping of cloister and college or money bag, but shall overflow to the nethermost portions of the earth at the command of the humblest heir of the divine intelligence.

Start from that as a low and where will you be in forty years? The Hays office and other leaders in the industry now use for general pronouncements a quieter and deeper note, and the advertising writers try occasionally to make an effect by setting down an unadorned statement of fact. More often they continue to cry out at the top of their bent. It does much to enrich the language: "Denied her birthright of love, she sought excitement in headlong romance, extravagant adventure, while her nation rose up to destroy its pampered darlings. Secret chapters torn from the life of the most glamorous woman who ever lived, filmed at cost of millions! Dazzling splendor! Star cast of thousands!"

"Here's a rousing drama of a beauty who walked right out of the Social Register into the crushing arms of a dare-devil lad from the slums of life. Packed with power! Racing with romance! Teeming with thrills!"

"The rebel genius life never tamed strides across the screen to become an immortal character in the motion picture gallery of the great!"

"An American Cavalcade! Through the pageantry of our own turbulent years, the vivid love story of three fine young people who fought their way from the honky-tonks of the Barbary Coast to the plaudits of the world today! A picture even greater than they say it is."

"Infuriated Brute, Vic McLaglen; Icy-Eyed Sadist Killer, Peter Lorre; Blood-Sucking Vampire, Bela Lugosi; Contemptible Cur, John Caradine."

"Sock! At the heart, at the funny bone, at the tear ducts, at the purse strings."

The advertising writer is at his most glorious when faced with the necessity of presenting a classic to the millions, when he is obliged, for instance, to convince them that Shakespeare is not only culture but a heart throb and a thrill, that, played by the right stars, his dramas can lift anybody out of his seat. Here is a summary of the big moments in "the greatest love story of all time," Norma Shearer and Leslie Howard in Shakespeare's *Romeo and Juliet:*

Love's Coming of Age—Beautiful Juliet is told by her parents that the time has come when she must seek a husband. *The Masque Ball*—Romeo in disguise. The grand ball of the Capulets. Pageantry. Music. Magnificence. Romeo finally meets the starry-eyed Juliet. *The Famed Balcony Scene*—Romeo climbs to the forbidden chamber where love waits—but where death threatens if he is discovered. *Stolen Kisses*—Feverish moments reveal their passion as the lovers say farewell on Juliet's moon-drenched balcony. *Lovers Reunited in Death*—Romeo drains the poison phial and falls beside his adored Juliet as the latter wakes from her sleeping potion. Beholding her lover dead beside her, Juliet plunges a dagger into her heart.

Of *A Midsummer Night's Dream* it was written: "First rendered by a cast consisting exclusively of male performers and entirely without scenery, its presentations have steadily increased in richness, culminating in Max Rheinhardt's brilliant outdoor production. And now on the infinite stage of the screen, Shakespeare and Rheinhardt at last find unlimited scope for the complete expression of their imaginative genius."

In this finding the elements of popular appeal in the classics the advertising man has become an ex-

pert. He works by no stereotyped method. When
Alexander Korda found most of his potential audience unaware of the identity of *Rembrandt* he
offered free passes to anyone who could prove that
he owned an authentic Rembrandt painting. Warner's advertising department think they pulled the
first audiences into *The Life of Emile Zola* by a
phrase in the trailer which showed people who had
never heard of him that this French author was a
man worth knowing: "He plucked from the gutter
a faded rose and made an immortal masterpiece."
For packed content, factual and emotional, that
sentence would be difficult to equal.

The producer of a stage play waits always with
a good deal of nervousness for the morning-after-
the-first-night comments of the critics. About the
critic's power, national or local, the motion picture
industry is inclined to be skeptical. A critic can
damn a film, some of them feel, but not sell one.
Others will deny his power either to save or damn.
At just one point, the evaluation of imported foreign language films, his word seems to be law. That
is probably because they get so comparatively little
advertising that the chief information to be found
about them is in the reviewers' columns. With all
home products, however, the industry thinks the
critic's strength negligible as compared to the
"grapevine." A publicity man once told me of a
stunt he hoped some day to persuade his company
to use, a scientific test of the grapevine's power:

Take a picture that you know is good and one that has all the elements of popular appeal. Do not advertise the picture at all. Run it at a theater where the usual admission price is fifty cents. Put the price for its first night down to twenty-five cents. You will get a fair audience just for the bargain. Next day jump the price to seventy-five cents and stay there for the rest of the run. The people who came the first night attracted by the bargain price will express their enthusiasm, over the grapevine, so convincingly that everyone else will rush to get in at any cost.

If the grapevine is mightier than advertising it is certainly mightier than the critics. "The box-office importance of newspaper criticism is exaggerated," says the *Motion Picture Herald* flatly, "and it's the theater man himself who is to blame. If the critic's opinion is so important how did he get that way? Mostly, through the consistent build-up he obtains in theater publicity and advertising from the exhibitor who three-sheets his reviews in advertisements and displays." It is an almost unavoidable temptation to dress up a second or third day's advertisement with "rave notices," and to some extent the practice is safe. More movie fans read the advertisements than the criticisms and the advertiser need not report the critic's unfavorable comments. Moviegoers will pay attention to the one, two, three stars a reviewer sets beside a picture, the poor, fair to excellent barometer, or whatever device he uses to indicate his estimate briefly, but when he launches into detailed reasoned exposition of his opinion the critic is often talking to himself alone. Most of the points on which he dwells seem to the exhibitor trivial. Only when he says something about the performance of a star, rates it as above or below her usual level, is he saying something the average moviegoer wants to hear. Otherwise the critic is useful chiefly for making an impression upon that section of the twenty-six million who rate as "intellectuals." They have respect for the metropolitan newspapers and the highbrow magazines. The critic has his uses as prestige but that is about all.

So the serious motion picture critic has a somewhat lonely time of it. His literary friends are inclined to pity him. They suggest encouragingly that some day he may work up to be a dramatic critic. They take it for granted that the theater, music, books will always command more respect than the film. The critic's friends in the industry think that he wastes his fire on inessentials or that he is deliberately showing off, posing as recondite, a "montage boy." Once in a while someone comes to his aid. Alistair Cook has gathered together some interesting examples of movie criticism and published them under the title of *Garbo and the Nightwatchman*. They make good reading, fresh, lively, because there is as yet no movie critical stereotype, and they come from the typewriters of men and women who understand both factors in the game, who know the importance of box-office and also of crosscutting,* who are convinced that to be popular a film does not need to be bad.

Just once a year it seems worth while to the industry to take the critics really seriously, that is when the New York men meet to determine the "bests" of the year. Anything they put on record then is clear gain from the advertising point of view. Their badge of approval is one more trophy with which to deck a star or one more reason why the provinces should see the season's big picture when it gets into the third- and fourth-run houses. It may not always be fourteen carat but for the good exploitation man gold is where you find it.

Many kinds of men are engaged in the serious business of exploiting the movies but none regard it more respectfully than the theater managers. "The theater manager," says Daryl Zanuck, "must exercise as much creative effort in designing his show, in exhibiting the picture, as we must put into the production of it."

The theater manager, says an important trade journal, when he fashions his campaigns "does more than spend money. He effects merchandising coöperations that stimulate retail business. He

---

* When two scenes are supposed to take place simultaneously and the camera moves from one to the other that is known as crosscutting. It is effective in producing contrast or suspense.

plants newspaper tie-ups that encourage reader activity and spending. He awakens healthy interest in school children by constructive contests. Through ingenious devices he brings crowds to shopping districts. The theater man profits thereby, of course, as do other businesses working with him. But only the showman's ideas and executions make possible this extra community activity."

Extra community activity is the great American ideal. American business is always happiest when it can think of itself as a civic servant and the theater man is buoyant when he is working in coöperation with the mayor or, better still, the governor. Under his tutelage our public officials are becoming more and more conscious of their obligations as sponsors of good art for the community. They may not quite realize it yet but, even though the approach is somewhat oblique, they are strengthening the growing national conviction that art for the people is one of the legitimate concerns of a government. When, for instance, it was desirable to make the country aware of its opportunity to see on the screen that enduring American classic *Tom Sawyer*, statesmen and exhibitors labored shoulder to shoulder all up and down the land. Mark Twain is buried in Elmira, New York. When the youthful stars of the picture, Tom Kelly and Ann Gillis, appeared in Elmira in person the Mayor received them on the steps of the City Hall and presented them with the keys of the city. They went to Texas. The Mayor of Dallas proclaimed a "Tom Sawyer Day" and made Tom Kelly Deputy Mayor for the duration of his visit. Not to be outdone the Governor of the state appointed Tom an honorary Texas Ranger and conferred on Ann the title of youngest Admiral in the Texas Navy. The tour swept triumphantly across the country. Only Mayor La Guardia was deaf to the call of patriotism; Tom was refused the keys to New York City despite the fact that he is a native son of the Bronx.

Judy Garland fared better. She chanced to be in her native Providence at the moment of the opening there of *Everybody Sing* and she consequently had her day as Honorary Governor of Rhode Island. She showed herself worthy of the trust by devoting her gubernatorial time to the promotion of education and religion. In the lobby of the theater which was showing her film she sold autographed copies of a local newspaper for the benefit of a college building fund and she sang *Ave Maria* at three church services on Sunday morning.

All public servants are eager to advance the cause of cinematic art. The commanding officer at Fort Douglas in Utah detailed a hundred and fifty men, accompanied by a band, to march through the streets of Salt Lake City for the opening there of *Yellow Jack*. The soldiers set up a lobby display of pup tents, cots, mess kits, and side arms and opened a recruiting station in front of the theater. The Governor of Louisiana issued a proclamation urging all his people to see *The Buccaneer*, whose locale is the New Orleans of 1812. The Governor of Missouri had *I'm from Missouri* privately screened for him in the executive mansion. The Governor of Kentucky, the Lieutenant Governor, and the mayors of Kentucky's chief cities went out to the coast, on the invitation of Twentieth Century-Fox, to attend the première of *Kentucky*. The Governor of Tennesee did not need even the spur of local patriotism. For art alone he drove from the Capitol to the Knickerbocker Theater in a car with the Seven Dwarfs. The Mayor of Albany proclaimed a "Snow White Week." The Governor of Delaware promoted municipal campaigns for housing and safe driving by attending a special screening of *Boy of the Streets*. The Mayor of Boston helped National Air Mail Week by going to the landing field to receive, for Loew's State Theater, the print of *Yellow Jack* which the MGM Studios sent on by plane from New York. The Illinois State Legislature passed a resolution calling for the appointment of a committee of seven senators and seven representatives to attend the Springfield première of *Young Mr. Lincoln*. One hundred and fifty mayors and governors issued proclamations signaling the advent of "Motion Pictures' Greatest Year."

Quite as keenly as his civic work the devoted

"Taking Hollywood to the nation" was started by Warner Brothers. They ran a special train from California to Oklahoma for the opening of "Dodge City."

Coöperating with the movies is becoming one of the duties of Government officials. The Governors of Colorado, Kansas, and New Mexico join the stars in a broadcast at the "Dodge City" première.

A step was taken which led to a program addressed less to fur implicitor. But... Denial from one in order to please another when...

theater manager enjoys coöperation with the schools. Whenever his bill includes a literary classic transferred to the screen he memorializes all the teachers and offers special rates to Shakespeare or Dickens classes if they care to take blocks of tickets. He will even go so far as to arrange for them a private showing of some particularly important film. For a special performance of *Heidi* almost any town is happy to turn its schools out at ten o'clock on any week-day morning. Where sufficient mutual good will has been established the theater man distributes "study guides" in advance of the showing of a history film like *Suez* or *Man of Conquest*. Often teachers will promise extra class credits to those who attend. A brisk and personable theater manager can help, too, by addressing the school chapel on the day of the opening of an historical picture or by providing the dramatic script for a program of excerpts from the film, to be delivered by students under the coaching of the teacher of public speaking. Managers have been known to offer prizes to the composition class for essays, to the art class for paintings having to do with some especially worthy film.

With the heavy task of the college, too, the theater manager is delighted to lend a hand. One especially effective piece of coöperation was reported by a theater man in Oklahoma who found himself running *A Yank at Oxford* just after the selection of Rhodes Scholars from the southwest district. Two students were appointed from the state university and the academic authorities arranged a ceremony in their honor. The English secretary of the Rhodes committee who was present was happy to see the film and to write a series of newspaper articles on the accuracy of its picture of Oxford life. All former Rhodes scholars on the university faculty were invited to the theater as guests of the management. The theater manager in Athens, site of the University of Georgia, decided that the sporting angle was the one to work in his community rather than the academic. He arranged for *A Yank at Oxford* a relay race between sixteen university fraternities, the contestants circling a city block and finishing in front of the theater. The winning fraternity was given a theater party and all the runners got free tickets.

With the church, too, the theater man is happy to coöperate whenever an opportunity offers. The San-Val Drive-in Theater near Los Angeles, for instance, has been "offered to all churches for Sunday services during any part of the day, free of any cost to the church. This has created very favorable comment from all factions." A manager in Wilkes-Barre, Pennsylvania, promoted a "go to church on Easter Sunday" campaign, took shots of local celebrities arriving at the churches, and showed them, properly advertised, at his theater during Easter week. A manager in Elroy, Wisconsin, arranged a special screening of *Boys Town* for the local clergy—and every one of them praised the film in church next morning. Still more subtle coöperation was obtained by an exhibitor in Thomasville, Georgia, who writes:

Some time ago, a Gypsy Smith tent revival hit us, and when he moves in you are really hit. We inserted the following in a small box in the weekly program: "The revival opens Sunday. Mr. Gypsy Smith has more to offer you than we have. This theater remains open, but not in a spirit of competition. If you want to see a picture, there will be one here for you, but there will be more for you at the tent. If you can't come to both, go to the revival."

I don't believe that this little spread got the revival a single person who would not have gone anyway, but it got us a column editorial in the local paper, Associated Press Stories, and best of all Gypsy Smith read it at a meeting attended by half the population, and spoke well of us from the pulpit. The audience applauded, and it undid the lifetime work of some fire-eating local preachers who had for years been advising their followers that the road to Hell was bordered by picture houses. It got us fifty new patrons, several of them zealots who had never seen a motion picture before.

By this sort of attachment of the film to civics, education, and religion the exhibitor is working in the forefront of the industry's campaign to bring into the theaters the other twenty-six million who do not yet go to the movies. The exhibitors are quietly showing that part of the twenty-six million who constitute the "intellectuals" how closely bound up the movies are with uplift and social betterment. In fact so eager have the theater men become in their pursuit of culture and civic good, in their savoring of the delights of dignity, that there is sometimes grave danger of their neglecting their obligation to the crowd, the eighty-five million who should never be forgotten and the larger section of the twenty-six. The Managers' Round Table, "an international association of showmen meeting weekly in *Motion Picture Herald* for mutual aid and progress," feels frequently constrained to remind its members of the importance of a quality it has felicitously named "boom-boom."

What is this picture business? Just another kind of show. And how do you put over a show? You beat on the drum. That's how they did it in the beginning, and no one ever thought up any smarter way of doing it yet.

What's happened to show business? They threw away the drum and bought a fiddle. But fiddles don't boom-boom. And you've got to have boom-boom if you want to have show business.

The Wilmer and Vincent circuit just threw away the fiddle and bought a drum. A big drum. Yes, at the annual convention, the W. and V. folks decided to make boom-boom again by reviving circus methods of exploitation. And it's about time. Not especially for W. and V., but for all exhibition. Circuses always made money with boom-boom. Pictures and circuses are closely related. The same bally goes for both. The bird who says "no" is talking to himself. There never was a time when pictures could prosper without a ceaseless barrage of boom-boom. Wasn't so long ago that the big drum raised all kinds of box-office dust. But then dignity came along. And you know what happened. No more boom-boom.

So they're throwing away the fiddles and buying drums. That's something. A drum makes a sweeter box-office noise than a fiddle. A fiddle goes "peep-peep." A drum goes "boom-boom."

It is in making boom-boom that the exhibitor shows, as Mr. Zanuck says, his creative talent. His business is not to criticize his medium but to work with it, to take the crude material, the finished film, and fashion from it lovely exploitations. Exploitation is a handmaid art which seems to be essential to the cinema. Without it the best of films might crumble and die in its tin.

A few of the principles of exploitation are obvious even to the amateur. In the best exploitations the idea springs from the film itself, either from its content or from its title. A good many small fires broke out in theaters playing *Too Hot to Handle.* A manager in Boston publicized *The Hurricane* by taking out hurricane insurance on his theater—and collecting it when the real tropic storm came up the coast and blew his canopy off. When burglars cracked the safe in the Winona,

Wisconsin, theater just before the opening of *Little Tough Guy* the manager led off all his advertisements with "What little tough guy cracked the safe in the Winona Theater?" Not everyone can tie in his exploitations quite so neatly but the ingenuity and fertility of the exhibitor making boom-boom are tireless. During a certain week in February every dentist and doctor's office in Kansas City received an anonymous telephone call. Be sure, said the voice at the end of the wire, to keep your copy of this week's *Life* on the top of the pile of magazines in your waiting room. *Life*, the dentists discovered, was featuring the *Goldwyn Follies* then showing in town.

A theater in Pampas, Texas, had its print of *Wells Fargo* carried two hundred and fifty miles on horseback from Oklahoma City by a girl dressed like a rider for the Pony Express.

A humanitarian manager in Washington, D. C., determined that everyone who loved dogs should have a chance to see the *Bob, Son of Battle* picture released as *To the Victor*. He printed quantities of those little sheets courageously known in the trade as "throwaways" and arranged to have one handed to every spectator at the National Capital Dog Show. He mailed them, too, to every pet shop, dog hospital, S.P.C.A., boarding kennels, breeder, and veterinarian in the city.

A New York theater stationed a special taxi outside during the run of *Sweethearts* and offered any couple who asked for it a free ride to the Marriage License Bureau. Twelve couples are reported to have been stirred by the film to get marriage licenses.

To advertise the Hardy family series Loew's in Boston arranged a contest, with judges from the School Committee and the Chamber of Commerce, in which letters were written on "Why the Hardys Should Live in Boston."

In Hartford, Connecticut, the print of *Jesse James* was carried from the station to the theater in a stagecoach. As the coach, attracting crowds on every corner, moved through the city, Jesse James and his band galloped out of a side street and held it up. They took the film and rode away. Immediately the coach was surrounded by newsboys shouting: "Extra, extra, Jesse James captured; now at Loew's Poli."

During the run of *Checkers* an upstate New York theater man who was an expert player challenged everybody in town and promised free tickets to anyone who could beat him. When *Gold Is Where You Find It* was played in Hammond, Indiana, the theater offered free seats to anyone who could show an authentic gold nugget mined in California. All girls named *Sally, Irene* or *Mary* got in free to that picture in Shawnee, Oklahoma, and a theater in Minneapolis offered twenty-five dollars to any girl who would attend *One Hundred Men and a Girl* with a hundred escorts. A New

England theater admitted free anyone coming on a bicycle to the opening performance of *A Yank at Oxford*, sure that they would applaud the bicycle sequence.

That *Yank at Oxford* was a film that lighted showmen's imaginations. It appealed to Rhodes scholars; it appealed to bicyclists; it appealed to the ladies. One theater offered six pairs of blue Oxfords to the six women writing the most interesting love notes to Robert Taylor. A local shoe store supplied the Oxfords.

That "tie-up" with local merchants is important. It is a vital part of the exhibitor's work, especially in the small town. The "tie-up" is one of the ways in which he "stimulates business" and "makes possible extra community activity." He may "promote" dress models to be shown on the stage or in the lobby when a picture stresses the heroine's wardrobe. He may serve "promoted" coffee and doughnuts from an old chuck wagon outside the theater where some epic of the Western plains is showing. Bakers like to make promoted cakes with any sort of legend on the icing. It is a mutual benefit arrangement. The public gets a few free cakes while the theater and the baker get a lot of nearly free advertising, each one doubling the range of his appeal and saving half the cost.

Sometimes a theater manager feels the need of an appeal beyond anything the film of the day has to suggest. It is then that he resorts to screeno and free dishes. The industry is inclined to frown on those devices. Even where lotteries are legal, and more and more judges are ruling against them, they are extraneous to art. Offering your patrons other reasons for coming to the theater besides seeing a movie may fill the seats temporarily but is likely to defeat its purpose in the long run. One catches in all discussion of these bribed-attendance devices the note of wounded artistic pride struggling against commerce. It is not possible that women should really prefer plates to pictures. An exhibitor is an artist, not the manager of a gambling joint.

A new method of exploitation, extraneous to the feature film but properly connected with the theater, is being experimented with by some energetic exhibitors—the local newsreel. The manager takes the pictures himself or enlists the aid of the local newspaper. Parades, high-school ball games, outdoor celebrations of any kind are good subjects but it is quite effective just to take pictures of shopping crowds in front of the principal stores or of school children at recess. "See yourself in the newsreel" is a slogan of great power. The idea can be carried further, for local celebrities are usually not averse to being photographed in characteristic action. Provident theaters file their local newsreels carefully away for anniversary revivals.

Other provident theater managers are at work conditioning the audience of tomorrow. The accepted method of training the young moviegoer is to form a "kiddie club." The local newspaper helps in recruiting members and the theater runs special shows for club members on Saturday mornings when they get for their dime admission not only a cartoon and a Western but an harmonica playing contest or a lollypop-pick-up game with really good prizes "promoted" from one of the local stores. On special holidays everybody in the audience is given promoted candy. Some clubs celebrate their members' birthdays; some send flowers to any member who is sick. One manager calls up every one of his kid club members on Friday afternoon to remind them of the Saturday show. His theory is that a kid feels pretty important when there's a telephone call for him and is almost certain to turn up at the theater next morning. Some of the managers are inclined to feel that the kids are not worth all this trouble but the men who take their business seriously are convinced that today's dimes will turn into the quarters of tomorrow.

Even when his audience, of any age, is at the doors the good exhibitor will not stop to draw breath. As they walk into the lobby they must be reassured that they have turned their steps in the right direction for an evening's entertainment. "Stills" must smile at them encouragingly, "cut-outs" and "blow-ups" beckon them on. And, lest cardboard should not be strong enough, the exhibitor will add, according to the title of the evening, a dilapidated stagecoach, a leopard—stuffed if he can do no better, a Louis XVI clock, or a costumed usher looking sadly through prison bars.

Most important of all lures are the pictures of the evening's stars, but the exploitation of the stars is a long and curious story. Part of it will be found in Chapter III, "Glamour."

Once he has them inside the theater the showman wants to make his patrons so comfortable that they will never be able to think of a better place to spend their evenings. Some of the best architectural, engineering, and decorative thought in the country is now going into the perfection of moving picture theaters, thought on the proper angle for seats, the best kind of cushions, the precise amount of light, the acoustically perfect ceiling, the number of decibels above the noise level of the theater to which the sound equipment must be tuned to produce the best emotional effect. When an audience sits enthralled and motionless through a big scene, like the iceberg sequence in *Spawn of the North*, the pitch is just right.

An elaborate scheme designed to make the patron feel that the movie theater is his natural home is the drive-in theater of which there are now some dozen scattered about the country with more to come. The big lots, capable of accommodating hundreds of cars, are arranged in an ingenious series of semicircular ramps which tilt the front of the car up as it comes into place so that occupants of both front and back seats have a perfect view of the screen. It is a large screen, fifty, sometimes sixty-five feet wide, so that the actors swell to twice the proportions they have in the usual theater. The ramps are so arranged that any car can go in or out without obstructing the vision of the spectators in any other car. If it rains you just shut the car windows and keep on looking. Either amplifiers are placed in the cars or the sound apparatus is geared to be heard through glass and cranking motors. The only thing that can interfere with a patron's comfort is fog.

The drive-in theater is not troubled by the problem of interior decoration which bulks large for the others. Is it better to offer elegance or just plain comfort? Will you do more business with old masters in the lobby or with air conditioning? The theaters which can afford it try both. When a movie theater really wants to be elegant there are few modern institutions that can compare with it. Consider, for instance, the Esquire Theater in Chicago as described in *Better Theatres*. It seats fifteen hundred and cost a half million to build.

The entire building was constructed so that every detail in it would appear to be a stage setting. A nonseasonal atmosphere has been established by the liberal use of ferns, shrubs, and artificial trees in and around the front.

The lobby is decorated in quiet tones, with a wood finish covering the entire wall. Music coming from hidden recesses permeates the lobby and all of the public rooms. This music is created by an automatic record changing phonograph and a radio, hooked to a speaker system, and serves to establish an entertainment mood in the mind of the patron, immediately cutting off the outside world.

The main staircase, leading to the balcony, is broken up by a series of landings and intimate nooks, so that those ascending the stairs will lose all conception of rising to any height. On one side of the balcony foyer is an intimate studio gallery, where the works of local artists and photographers are displayed from time to time.

The seats are of the new "Push-Back" type. Luxuriously upholstered, even to the arms, the seats move back to allow easy passage between rows.

All ushers, as well as the maid, carry cigarettes and matches which are offered to all people. When a holdout* has been in effect for any length of time, the candy case attendant, an attractive young lady, and the directorette, offer those waiting a tray of cooling mints and a glass of sparkling Waukesha water.

At the end of each performance, the waterfall curtain is lowered, and the house lights raised for a two or three minute intermission. There is never any "speed up" for turnover purposes. From the start to the finish the performance unreels in leisurely fashion. This is the cue to the entire operation of the theater.

Another solicitous manager in Saratoga Springs solved for his patrons the eat-your-cake problem.

* A holdout is ordered when the theater is full and newcomers cannot be seated before the beginning of the next show.

He stated at the top of a summer advertisement that "a fortune" had been invested in "equipping for your cool comfort" his air-conditioned theater, and on the next line that the current film provided "blazing tropic adventure to storm your heart and soul." When Radio City Music Hall found that it was sweeping up more handkerchiefs after each showing of *Dark Victory* than had been collected since the moist days of *Little Women*, back in 1933, it was arranged to keep the house lights down a few seconds longer so that the feminine members of the audience could wipe away their tears in private. A thoughtful manager in Detroit has already given his patrons a foretaste of the "feelies" which Aldous Huxley scheduled for our future in *Brave New World*. He adjusted his cooling system so that the audience felt a faint suggestion of mist during the storm scenes in *The Hurricane*.

Against this ceaseless, subtly unpredictable beat of boom-boom what chance has the average citizen to protect himself? He walks down Main Street in the evening not as a free agent, simply as a puppet at the mercy of a little art working in the service of a big art, the art of exploitation laboring in the interests of the art of the movies.

III

GLAMOUR

THE natural American spelling of glamour would be g-l-á-m-o-r, with the accent on the first syllable. Hollywood spells it with a u, accenting the last syllable and drawing it out as long as possible, whether in derision or enthusiasm—glamóur. Glamour might be defined as, first and most important, sex appeal (though that phrase is banned by the Hays office, you have to say "it" or "oomph"), plus luxury, plus elegance, plus romance. Glamour is at present an accepted stock, and a very important stock in trade in the movie business. But is it on the wane? Is the era of glamour over? Does glamour no longer pay? There are those who think that its power to move the multitudes is weakening.

One or two eminent authorities, men who ought to know, have come out flatly for glamour's death. Not that they wish it themselves—no producer ever tells you what he wishes—but they feel that the public does. Warner Brothers' official position is anti-glamour. They sell, they say, not stars but stories; what the public now wants is not luxe but action and fast plots. Samuel Goldwyn, while allowing that ladies may still be glamorous, thinks the fashion has gone out for men. He took pains to present the masculine star of *The Hurricane* as a youth quite free from any suspicion of the cloying charm. When Jon Hall was sent on a quick tour of the country for the purpose of being interviewed by the press in various cities the publicity agent who accompanied him made a point of telling the newspapers that Jon owned just one suit of clothes and that had been tailored for the trip. The tuxedo in which he appeared on necessary formal occasions was borrowed from the studio wardrobe. Jon Hall, the story ran, is just a typical American boy who happens to be working for his living in pictures instead of hardware. More significant, because his box-office power is so much greater, is James Stewart whose publicity includes such "overheard in the lobby" remarks as: "He's a real American type, the kind I'd like to have around the house"; and "Reminds me of how my Frankie makes love, so modest like."

In the spring of 1938 the Independent Theater Owners' Association, Inc., of New York City rocked the country by inserting in the *Hollywood Reporter* a red-bordered advertisement announcing that they were tired of losing money on expensive stars who no longer had any box-office appeal. They advised the producers to concentrate on making good pictures. "We are not against the star system, mind you, but we don't think it should dominate the production of pictures." The stars whom they listed specifically as no longer of interest to the public were all of them glamour girls. The discussion became a personal matter of course, an attack and defense of the public power of certain personalities, but it swung wide beyond those narrow bounds. Newspapers debated it pro and con. Magazines proved their points with photographs. It became in time a metaphysical question: Can glamour die? Or is glamour eternal? Is it only the elements of glamour that change?

Certainly the elements have altered, even in the short span of decades by which the movies measure their life. One of the earliest national idols was Theda Bara, the first screen "vamp." Today that thrilling word vamp has lost all power to move except to laughter. There is a publicity picture of Theda Bara, made in 1916, which shows her seated on the ground, her knees drawn up, her elbows extended, stiff, her chin resting on her clasped hands. Before her, on its back, lies a human skeleton. She is the fatal woman, the woman whose love drives men mad, drives them to drink and suicide and crime. She looks down at her work. Skeletons and skulls were an important part of the vampire aura.

Theda was the first star to receive a thorough publicity "build-up" in the modern manner. Born Theodosia Goodman she had shortened her name for stage purposes to Theda and evolved Bara by contracting a relative's name, Barranger. This seemed to her press agents far too credible to be interesting. They announced that she was the daughter of a French artist by his Arabian mistress, that she had been born on the desert sands, that Bara was an anagram—Arab spelt backward, and Theda a rearrangement of the letters of death. At her first big interview, in Chicago, when she was en route from New York to California, Theda Bara received reporters in a darkened room in the Blackstone Hotel. The walls were hung with black and scarlet, the air was heavy with incense and tuberoses. Theda, very pale, in trailing garments of black and scarlet, reclined on a couch and spoke languidly with an Arabian-French accent. The reporters had never seen anything like it before; they were enormously impressed. The Chicago papers carried columns about the fascinating and devastating vamp.

The fatal tigress fashion waned with the Great War. Glamour as we know it today was really invented, or better, discovered, by Cecil DeMille and his continuity writer, Jeanie MacPherson. They noted that the two chief interests of men and women during the postwar boom were sex and money, and they proceeded accordingly. Everybody was making money. Enormous fortunes were being amassed overnight and even people in the lower brackets were piling up what looked like fortunes compared to what they had had before. Everybody was interested in ways of spending money. The new rich, whether they counted their income in hundreds or in thousands, wanted to know all about high-powered cars, airplanes, ocean liners, yachts, villas, exotic food, wine, jewels, Paris dresses, perfect servants; and DeMille told them. His were really the first educational films.

Then fact and fiction played into each other's hands. Stars' salaries increased and audiences were delighted when they found that the marvelous beings whose progress through luxury they admired on the screen enjoyed similar pleasures in their daily lives. The dream that began in the theater need have no interruption at all. It could go on all day as well as all night. The publicity agents who succeeded Theda Bara's were more subtle and a bit more truthful; they did not manufacture personalities quite out of thin air; they took the facts and bathed them in a rich warm light. They fanned the coals of glamour and it flamed all through the 1920's. In the '30's came a change.

The place to study glamour today is in the fan magazines, but no one unaccustomed to fan literature should enter upon a course of it without a doctor's certificate. Fan magazines are distilled as stimulants of the most exhilarating kind. Everything is superlative, surprising, exciting; everybody is always having a wonderful time, or else recounting with great gusto the details of a desperate early struggle or overwhelming catastrophe met with a fighting courage which led swiftly to the giddy heights of glamour. Nothing ever stands still; nothing ever rests, least of all the sentences. Fan magazine writers employ a special vocabulary of telescoping phrases; they leave out all possible connectives; they eschew relative clauses; they beat upon the reader with adjectives—and he comes back for more. The trained reader loves it. It can jar him, or more often her, out of the most sodden of weekend lethargies. There are about a score of fan magazines and their circulation runs from two hundred thousand to a million. That is a small figure set beside the eighty-five million weekly attendance at the movies but not every moviegoer can be a fan; to be a fan is almost a profession.

A study of current fan magazines will make it immediately apparent that the most important thing for a glamorous star to have today is personality. The insistence on this in the midst of a standardized society is touching. The moviegoers who insist on dressing like everyone else yet cherish a desire to look distinguished. They conform meticulously to pattern in the purchase of cars, houses, furniture, food; they are desperately afraid of being unfashionable or incorrect, and yet they yearn to be individuals. They pay Dale Carnegie and Emily Post or their lesser imitators round sums to show them how to develop their personalities, and admire extravagantly the woman who dares to be herself, though of course she must keep her differences within certain well-prescribed limits. Though they are perfectly well aware that they share their escape personalities with thousands of others it still seems to them essential that those personalities should be "different."

If she is individual the admired star need not be extravagantly beautiful. The ranking box-office favorites must be good to look at certainly but they are not required to be creatures of classic perfection. In many ways it is an advantage for a star not to be too beautiful. She stands then closer to the average and that is what the fans want, an ideal that they can emulate, a creature not too bright and good, one whose heights they might actually scale themselves, given a little energy and a little luck. Glamour should never be so bright that it dims hope. That is Janet Gaynor's great appeal: her home-town girl personality, the little blonde from the typewriter or the kitchen or the ribbon counter who has exchanged her imitation lapin coat for sables, her hall bedroom for a Beverly Hills villa, her Woolworth jewelry for real diamonds. The glamorous star today is as natural as possible. She does not pluck her eyebrows and paint in new ones; she develops the natural line. She does not tint her hair to exotic hues. She does not try to be a fairy-tale princess but an average American girl raised to the nth power. "Vivid" is the adjective she works for hardest.

There is another compliment to which she has no objection, "fabulously wealthy." It is better, though, to imply that than to say it. Enormous salaries are not quite so much talked about as they were in the '20's. Still it pleases a fan to read that Joan Crawford has made a new contract at $1,500,000 for three pictures a year, or that Carole Lombard pays, gladly, an income tax of $400,000, or that it cost Joan Blondell $100,000 to have a baby. Money is never unpleasant to contemplate even as cold cash but it fires the imagination better when transmuted into other forms. Glamour is founded upon an income but real glamour seldom looks at the bill.

The readers of fan magazines drink down their luxury straight or vary the brew with fiction. Originally devoted to "news" about the stars, the fan magazines have begun to add short stories, signed by popular names and dealing of course with the movies. They are full of paragraphs like this:

"Katrine Mollineux and Bill Naughton had been drinking champagne cocktails for most of the afternoon. He ducked suddenly, as Katrine threw a glass at him. It crashed, with a little silvery tinkle, against a marble column that had come from Pompei."

And this:

"We were in her bedroom before dinner and she was wearing blue velvet—she loved velvet and wore it often—and there was a new maid. The great jewel case lay open and the maid pressed a small spring and one compartment came open and there upon a white velvet bed was the smiling blue ring."

But the luxe of fact is really better than the luxe of fiction. At Warner Baxter's house, for instance:

The secretary sits in her small efficient office. A red button lights up. "What do you want?" she addresses it severely. Five hundred yards away, down by the big iron gate, her voice echoes eerily out of the trees and a delivery man with rosebushes on his wagon jumps backwards in surprise. Into the air he nervously explains his business. Five hundred yards away Miss Carr presses a button. The wrought-iron gates swing noiselessly open.

Or, Dolores Del Rio's gift to Gary Cooper's baby was "a tiny cross of baguette emeralds suspended from a platinum chain of exquisite workmanship."

Or, Madeleine Carroll won the heart of the wealthy, fascinating British Captain Philip Astley who presented her with "a swanky flat in Mayfair, a country castle outside of London, and a villa on an estate in Italy where she was married with all the peasants crowding around the private chapel."

Or, Sonja Henie has been decorated by the King of Norway.

Or, Bing Crosby breeds race horses.

Or, Shirley Temple has two hundred and fifty dolls.

Or, Joan Crawford has a famous collection of sapphires and diamonds. It can go on as long as you like.

Clothes of course are endlessly pictured and described, usually with marble fountains, private swimming pools, or limousines in the background. Every possible article is discussed from Irene Dunne's "deceptively simple" black frocks to the two-fingered glove designed by a famous maker because "his glamorous patrons frequently complained that it was most difficult to pull their gloves over their jeweled fingers."

Every aspect of life, trivial and important, should be bathed in the purple glow of luxury and now the aura of glamour can follow a star even beyond life's bounds. Almost as obligatory as a villa in Beverly Hills is the purchase today of a mortuary chamber—cost about $25,000—in Forest Lawn Memorial Park, America's most glamorous cemetery.

However thick the luxury in which a star is lapped, she takes care today to make it known that she is really a person of simple wholesome tastes, submitting to elegance as part of her job but escaping from it as often as possible. It soothes the fans to believe that luxury is fundamentally a burden. They like to hear that Warner Baxter has to nerve himself to go through with a formal dress-up party, one of those parties where his "long oak dinner table is stately with its ivory-colored *broderie anglaise* and filet lace cloth, the beautiful old silver, the ivory candles in the branched silver candelabra, the flat bowl of red roses, and the finely traced amber glass," while "deft service is rendered by the English butler." What Warner really prefers is simple informal parties in the summerhouse.

He particularly liked the summerhouse; anyone would. He liked the big, comfortable, three-sided sitting room, its fourth side open to the green swimming pool. He liked the snug little bar on one side, the remote-control radio, so that they could dance after dinner if they felt like it, the open fire and the charcoal-broiled steaks that he himself cooked on the iron grill. And he liked to putter around in the diminutive all-electric kitchen making some of his famous chile con carne.

It is nice to know, too, that Gary Cooper's "favorite article of apparel is a cheap pair of seersucker pants which he swiped from the wardrobe when he was working in *Now and Forever* a few years ago." Or that William Powell sold his quarter-milliondollar house because its "Georgian grandeur" was too much for him. It had tennis courts "of Grecian

Deanna Durbin's parents answer their own door-
bell. Or that the personal wardrobe of Kay Francis,
the screen's best-dressed woman, contains fewer
clothes than an extra's. "I do want to assure you,"
writes the editor of one of the more elegant fan
magazines to a worried reader, "that we do try
conscientiously and constantly to give you these
gallant people as they really are—living, experienc-
ing human beings who, underneath all their glitter
and beauty, are very much like you and me."

This desire to bring the stars down to earth is
one of the trends of the times. The films are cater-
ing to it as well as the fan writers. Each glamorous
lady must now be presented to her public in some
absurd or, preferably, painful, position. Not too
painful, of course; the audience wants to exult, not
to sympathize. The historic shot was fired in 1931
when James Cagney hit Mae Clarke in the eye with
a grapefruit but the world was not yet ready for
the change. Only in 1938 did the movement really
get under way. Today a star scarcely qualifies for
the higher spheres unless she has been slugged by
her leading man, rolled on the floor, kicked down-
stairs, cracked over the head with a frying pan,
dumped into a pond, or butted by a goat. Carole
Lombard, the archetype of heroines who can take
it, got her training in Mack Sennett comedies.

decline of masculine chivalry. Has it any political significance? Certainly it shows a desire to fetch glamour down from the realms of the utterly unattainable, to make it something on which the mere mortal can rest his hand.

To float near earth, very close to the average level, is even more important for the child star than for the glamour girl. The youthful actor must never be a prodigy, always just a regular kid. No checks in six figures, no birthday gifts from queens, no twenty-two-foot statue of herself in the city park must distract a little girl's attention from the delights of dolls and jump ropes. Shirley Temple also likes to concoct pies of mud and sawdust. She sells them to passing motorists. Jane Withers' house is overrun with pets but her mother doesn't mind; it helps to keep the child simple and unspoiled. The Mauch twins, "dressed in old sweaters and disreputable cords, reeking of shellac and turpentine," make presents for their mother out of redwood and mahogany. Freddie Bartholomew has two dogs and likes swimming and football. The film children are strictly regulated also as to pocket money, often no more than a dollar a week, though most of them are supporting a line of relatives, attached for their sakes to studio pay rolls, and are investing against their own old age.

The young stars carry a heavy spiritual as well as financial burden. They must embody not only the dreams of their contemporaries who long for talent and curls and fame but also all the dreams of all the parents who have transferred their reveries from themselves to their children. The woman who has abandoned hope of any glamorous existence of her own can still escape from reality by identifying her drab-haired offspring with the happy creatures that flit across the screen, provided the difference between them is not *too* marked. For the sake of the mothers the child actors must remain just children even as for the sake of everybody their glamorous elders must express a preference for hash and overalls.

Actually simplicity is one of the easier virtues the glamorous stars have to practice. Their patrons exact from them a very high standard of morality. No star can be permitted to succeed simply by virtue of beauty or brains or talent. That would be to separate her too far from her admirers, to set up standards they could never reach. But anyone, by the American creed, can cultivate moral force. Success should be a product of the pioneer virtues. *A Star Is Born*, that best-to-date story of the industry, was very sound in making its little heroine take after grandmother who had crossed the plains in a covered wagon. Courage, energy, hard work, the refusal to be disheartened by difficulties, these are qualities that America still cherishes and she insists on finding them in her ideal men and women. The fan magazines sprinkle through the life stories of the stars sentences like these:

"Madeleine Carroll never makes the mistake of whining, so no one realizes that she, too, has had troubled hours."

"Gary Cooper is so darned humble and honest about himself he still to this day doesn't believe he has a thing any other guy hasn't."

"Allan Jones had a good Welsh background, strong, plain food, the Golden Rule, an honest wage honestly earned."

"Robert Montgomery says: 'I share with Rhodes his feeling when dying, he said, "So much to do, so little done." ' " (It is uncertain whether that version of Tennyson is Montgomery's or Rhodes'.)

"Robert Taylor was so considerate of other people on his trip aboard the *Berengaria* that the stewards became his fans to a man. They guarded his stateroom when he asked not to be disturbed, when he was writing a letter, for instance, or having his daily ocean phone talk with his mother."

"Bette Davis can meet the big things in life like a thoroughbred. Whatever her faults they do not include flinching in the face of catastrophe."

The virtues, true simplicity, personality, and rich helpings of magnificence have long been ingredients of glamour. Now there are new elements. It is possible today, for instance, to be glamorous and mature. "Glamour Begins at Thirty" a fan magazine heads an article on Claudette Colbert, and a newspaper reporter is permitted to list the stars of ten years ago who are still going strong. Nor is it now necessary for a lady to conceal the fact that she is a mother. Two, three, even four children are the accepted thing in Hollywood. The arrival of Margaret Sullavan's daughter was officially permitted to disrupt the casting of *Stage Door*. Indeed so far has the pendulum swung that those stars who have no children are adopting them. Newspapers are printing paragraphs like this:

"Irene Dunne and her husband, Dr. Francis Griffin, have adopted a four-year-old orphan who has been in their care for the last year. The child, blonde and blue-eyed, will be called Mary Frances Griffin."

"Pamela Bascom, thirteen-year-old orphan of Pomona, Cal. has become the protégée of Bette Davis and her husband, Harmon O. Nelson. Pamela has a coloratura soprano voice and dances well."

Miriam Hopkins has taken on a Michael; Constance Bennett a Peter; and it can be stated in print that "it is well known in filmdom's capital that a birthday party to which are invited the very young members of the colony is likely to take precedence over all other social events."

Even further from the original base of glamour are two new qualities: culture and an interest in serious social problems. If a star in the 1920's dressed expensively to suit her type, drove a high-powered car, rode fearlessly, and swam well it was not at all necessary to assure the public that her

Hollywood villa had a library or that she knew
something of art and music; but just run through
a fan magazine today:

"There is little of philosophy, psychology, matters political or sociological, that Bob Montgomery
has not read and studied. He is Duco-ed with the
drawing-room manner. He might, superficially,
seem to fit in with the Hemingways, the Noel
Cowards, all the Bright Young People. But he can
also hold his own with scientists, engineers, medical men, learned professors."

"Bette Davis as a child read everything. She read
the books of Louisa M. Alcott. She read *The Five
Little Peppers*, the *Little Colonel* books. She read
Grimms' Fairy Tales. And her mother read her
the classics, Dickens, Scott, Bulwer-Lytton, Stevenson, Bret Harte."

Rochelle Hudson could "give up the picture
business and still have a hundred ways in which to
keep myself interested every minute—music, dancing, painting, any number of things."

Anita Louise has "my other career, my harp. I
work quite as hard, quite as conscientiously at that
as I do at my work in the studio. I think it's bad
business to put all of your eggs in one basket."

Ronald Colman has "a well-stocked library,
which he uses. When a point of fact is disputed,
Colman can generally make straight for the page
in the book that settles the argument. He is interested in what interests most thinking men—his

work, his inner life, the state of the world which at the moment depresses him deeply."

Basil Rathbone "moves with the brilliant smart set. He talks of the really interesting things in foreign lands because he travels frequently."

The academic environment—Oxford—in which Heather Angel was "raised was responsible for her deep devotion to the dramatic classics, and resulted in her choice of the screen as a career. Shakespeare was studied by little Heather along with her A B C's."

Deanna Durbin reads "over thirty books a year."

Barbara Stanwyck "enjoys serious things—a lake by Corot, a book by Thackeray."

Ray Milland says, "I like astronomy, love to ponder on the composition and possibilities of the planets. My favorite book now is one on plant life as it's supposed to be on the moon. It's keen. Besides that, right now I'm wading through twenty-four volumes of the *Encyclopedia Britannica*."

In the last few years the interest of the Hollywood colony in social questions has been growing. "Bite of Political Bug" the Los Angeles *Times* called it in a banner headline, and the bite resulted in such unexpected activities as telegrams to the Governor of California asking him to pardon Tom Mooney, money for the Salinas lettuce strikers, the running out of town of Vittorio Mussolini and Leni Riefenstahl, the formation of an anti-Nazi league, publishing a newspaper and making radio

"He-man" qualities are very important to a masculine star. Tyrone Power is demonstrating them here while William Powell exhibits the serious interest in books which today is one of the elements in glamour.

"Happy Easter" from Ilona Massey to her fans. Members of fan clubs get season's greetings like this from their idols.

broadcasts, a Motion Picture Artists Committee raising thousands for Loyalist Spain, and, most significant perhaps of all, the winning of a closed shop for screen actors.

These activities, reported at length in the *New Republic* and *New Masses*, reach the fan magazines in somewhat diluted form. Luise Rainer, we are told, spends her time in New York visiting hospitals and slums and children's courts, but she does it partly from love of humanity and partly for the sake of her art. It is made very clear that she does not share the only too well-known radical opinions of her husband, Clifford Odets.

Deanna Durbin is a pacifist. She showed a reporter her school history book with a paragraph which she had underlined with red pencil. "It was Nicholas Murray Butler's estimate that for the money spent on the World War every family in ten countries could have had a $2,500 house, $1,000 worth of furniture, several acres of land [and so on]. 'Isn't it dreadful?' said Deanna. 'Not so much the money, as the millions of people killed.'" Ten years ago such a statement would not have added to the glamour of a youthful star, but at least it is safely away from present conflicts.

Gary Cooper is starting a coöperative ranch, to be run by his cowboy friends when they are not working in films. "This venture is an experiment to test the soundness of coöperative cattle raising." That is a pretty definite statement, though the cowboy and friendship elements tone it down a little.

Robert Montgomery's "real interests are in heavy matters, such as Guild shops for actors and writers, the promotion of better working conditions for every member of his own profession, beginning with extras. He is interested in providing for old-timers in pictures, old-timers who want work and can't get it. He is against censorship of all kinds. And does things about it." Guilds and censorship mentioned right out loud in a fan magazine, with an interest in them offered as an addition to a fine young man's glamour.

Certainly these differences in the make-up of glamour indicate a shift in the emphasis of society but to see them as marking the disintegration of a national commodity is probably to proceed too fast. No capitalist civilization, measuring success by material possessions, can afford to abandon completely the refreshment of release by identification with an ideal personality, the necessity for escape by dreams. Nothing less than a guillotine is likely to cut off the heads of the stars. Glamour will probably be with us for several years to come.

To examine it a little further, then, how is the shining fabric created? Screen publicity has two factories, New York and Hollywood. They do not love each other. New York publicity works on a comparatively rational basis. Hollywood must cater to the most fantastic community in the world. In a town which banks in Romanesque churches, eats in derby hats, opens a fruit stand with searchlights and sirens, gets gas from polar bears or Cleopatra's needle, the most imaginatively lavish behavior will scarcely keep a head above the milling crowd. A star must dress strikingly, drive an expensive car, be seen at the right places, put on spectacular parties, or even his own company may think he is slipping. He has both to hold his own where he is and keep making an impression all round against the day when he may want a contract from somebody else. A national reputation is not much helped by constant appearance in Hollywood papers or even in certain syndicated gossip columns or radio chitchats which everybody gets into, but Hollywood thinks it is important and a star who is left out, even by his own choice, suffers. The rising star may really prefer a quiet life, may want to stay at home in the evenings and save his salary, but the publicity office will have none of it. Working hours are not all spent at the studio. Any quiet game of cards with a few friends may be interrupted by a telephoned command to put in an appearance at such a restaurant at such an hour and to order champagne. The publicity department has seen to it that a photographer will happen by and that a particularly important glamorous lady will condescend to sit briefly at the table of the aspiring hero. Not until she has set her footprints in the forecourt of Graumont's Chinese Theater can a star even begin to express her publicity preferences.

Just fifty immortals so far have been permitted to make their marks in the wet concrete. Most of the marks are footprints but Al Jolson went down on his knees in memory of *Sonny Boy* and Sonja Henie cut two deep grooves with her skates.

Some of the picture posing business is of course for national as well as Hollywood consumption. Correspondents must be fed, and there are in Hollywood more than three hundred correspondents, for the fifteen or twenty fan magazines, for newspapers, syndicates, even the "quality" periodicals. They send news to all the United States and to twenty-four foreign countries. Even the Vatican has its correspondent in Hollywood. It has been estimated that one-hundred-thousand typewritten words a day go out of the city. Hollywood is the third largest news source in the country, outranked only by Washington and New York. A star of any magnitude must get into the important fan magazines at least once every three or four months; she really ought to be mentioned in some way, a picture or a gossip note, every month in the year.

A careful study of fan magazine illustration reveals that the importance of a star can be measured inversely by the amount of leg shown in her photographs. She mounts the ladder by way of sun bath and swimming pool poses. Not until she is safely at the top can she take to hostess gowns. Stories are even more trouble than pictures. Stories require "angles" and the strain upon publicity men and fan magazine writers who try to find them is terrific. Gilding lilies goes on twenty-four hours a day.

No wonder the Hollywood legend is fantastic, but it extends practically no distance at all beyond the truth. No explorer has yet returned to shatter it, though explorers have landed in Hollywood in every state of mind, as conquerors, as spies, as enthusiastic partisans, gaping yokels, or dispassionate observers. They go home to write their pieces in anger, excitement, laughter, or disillusion but they all add up to the same thing—there is no city like it on earth, thank heaven. So wide has the legend spread that the most casual traveler does not feel that he has been to California if he has not crossed the boundaries of Hollywood. Just to have driven through its streets is a privilege and to unlock a studio portal is to have material for talk for months. The most devoted bands of pilgrims are probably the members of fan tours organized by one or another of the magazines. The tours are skillfully planned, rates and dates within range of the clerk or stenographer who has been saving for months and months for this two weeks of glamour.

The tours cover all the natural wonders of California which any railroad would show you but they promise something more, "thrill-packed hours in the glamorous Hollywood of your dreams." "Want to know the details! After registering at the luxurious Clark Hotel, Movieland Tourists will spend the afternoon of the first day (Sunday) making a tour of Hollywood itself, where you will see the homes of the great film stars and other fascinating never-to-be-forgotten sights. Later in the afternoon you will be guests of Mr. and Mrs. Basil Rathbone, famous for their swanky filmland parties, for cocktails in their elaborate home. Sunday night will find Tourists visiting the famous Eddie Cantor broadcasts, where the popular Eddie and his youthful protégés, Deanna Durbin and Bobby Breen, will personally greet you. Monday morning Tourists are honored guests at the famous Paramount studios, where many of your favorite pictures are made. There you will accomplish what practically no other Hollywood visitors do—visit actual sets and watch pictures actually being made. Then you will have lunch in the Paramount restaurant, along with Claudette Colbert, Bing Crosby, Martha Raye, Fred MacMurray, Frances Farmer, and the other famous players who are 'in production' at that time." Another cocktail party, a preview in the studio projection room. "Tuesday morning you will visit the Max Factor Beauty Salon, where many of the great stars are made up for the screen, where the genial Mr. Factor himself will greet you. Then Tuesday night our Movieland Tourists will be feted at the Wilshire Bowl, playground of the stars, along with scores of famous Hollywood personalities. Warren Hull, handsome screen hero, will be master of ceremonies and there will be plenty of opportunities to get your autograph albums crammed with famous screen auto-graphs."

Such eagerness is there for these opportunities to see the great in person and to get their auto-graphs that the concerns that organize them thrive while the studios are put to continual inconven-ience with hardly tangible return. The Hollywood tour has taken on something of the proportions of a racket. Once in a while the victims rebel. When 159 members of the Jane Withers Fan Club of Chicago reached the doors of Twentieth Century-Fox one busy morning they found them shut. They were in despair until Warner Brothers' Studio heard the story and hurried down to capture the delegation and entertain them on their own lot. The Jane Withers Fan Club promptly offered to rechristen themselves in appropriate honor of some Warner Brothers' star.

Fortunately for those who make the films not many of the weekly attendants at the movies can get to Hollywood and try actually to touch their dreams. Most of the eighty-five million must feed their reveries with newsprint. The fan magazines are very good to them; they supply just those bits of information which the screen has no time to give; they make it possible for the worshiper to identify herself with the glamorous star as she can do with no other character in fiction. When you read a book you know only what the author tells you about the heroine, even though you follow her through sequel after sequel. On the stage you may not see the same actress once in five years but on the screen you can watch her over and over again, in different poses against scores of different backgrounds, and then you can follow her into the fan magazines. They will fill in for you all the little intimate details that make a personality real, that make identification close and exciting.

One obvious way to resemble your ideal is to dress as she does and no fan magazine is complete without its fashion department devoted to the costumes of the stars both on and off the screen. The glamorous ladies are less concerned here with displaying their latest purchases than with expounding their philosophy of dress, adaptable to a fifteen as well as a fifteen-hundred-a-week income, or showing what three outfits they consider fundamental to a perfect week-end.

Step two in intimacy is beauty hints. How does one's idol develop that copper sheen in her hair, that sparkle in her eye, that lovely contour of her leg? So seriously do the fans take advice, so conscientiously do they copy their models that publicity men can no longer indulge in flights of fancy about baths in goat's milk and honey, lotions compounded at the waning of the moon, or exquisitely imaginative reducing diets. Every beauty hint must now be checked by an expert lest the fan sicken in her enthusiastic imitation—and sue. The trend of the '30's, too, is away from cosmetics toward

s are full of
osity about
homes of
r favorite
. They en-
them as
m palaces or
o copy them
their own
and bunga-
. Bette Da-
garden, Paul
ni's living
n.

or his huckleberry pie. Domestic details are also useful to comedians, particularly to a character actor like Edward Everett Horton. His fan mail consists of letters from women who tell him how much he resembles their husbands.

Most subtle intimacy building device of all is the article on what the star is really like down underneath the glittering exterior he or she must wear for society as well as for the screen. Women adore the feeling that they are being confided in, that the world admires but they alone understand. A beneath-the-surface story, when it can be worked, probably goes further than anything else to attach a fan to a star. The fact that several hundred thousand other people are reading it at the same time is overlooked. Sometimes the story is the revelation of a private sorrow or a secret burden nobly and gaily borne. Sometimes it is the confession of a longing to retire to a life of obscure and quiet peace, to step out of the glare of the spotlight so bravely endured for the nation's good. Sometimes it is an interest in a serious pursuit with which professional engagements interfere. It is exciting to discover, for instance, that Rochelle Hudson is not really fluffy and domestic at all but a tigress; that under the "frills and foibles" of Billie Burke "there beats a big, bright brain"; that Glenda Farrell "on the screen, can take a guy for his last match box, but in real life, she can't get today's cocktail"; that "to be stared at, pointed out, buzzed over, makes the handsome Ronald Colman flinch with an almost physical distaste"; that what Leslie Howard really wants is not to act but to write.

Characters with hidden depths are rich in glamour but only very rarely is it possible to suggest that a star is actually quite different from the people she plays on the screen. The whole glamour system depends upon the identity of star and role. To the majority of spectators the stars are not so much actors as *alter egos*, or at least close personal friends, and to see them behaving out of character is to see one's universe rock, to feel one's personality dim, a sensation not unlike going mad. Not stupidity or lack of invention but rich human kindness makes the producers turn out picture after picture of the William Powell or Robert Montgomery, the Myrna Loy or Carole Lombard type. Reformers who think to improve the artistic quality of the movies by educating producers and directors should realize that they are reckoning without their host. Box-office, right at this point, definitely conditions art.

Instances of the identification of star and role are thick to hand. Consider for instance this statement by the manager of a theater in a small Minnesota town: "To me, *Sing, You Sinners* was ruined by about 200 feet of film showing Crosby intoxicated. I don't know how you or your patrons feel about scenes dealing with the star getting intoxicated, but I do know that about 75 per cent

attracting as much attention as they can from a
populace who might otherwise remain in ignorance
of the glory passing through their midst. The fans
make systematic attacks, too, upon the desk at the
star's hotel asking loudly for the opportunity to
get an autograph and so suggesting to others to do
the same.

Even in the idol's absence it is possible to spread
his fame. The Bing Crosby Club of Ramseur,
North Carolina, for instance, is a local power because it represents 40 per cent of the population.
They forced the city fathers to rename an important thoroughfare Crosby Street.

Fan clubs are useful not only to the established
but to the aspiring actor. The enthusiasts for the
novice bombard the powers in Hollywood with
letters expressing admiration for their idol and en-
treating that she may be seen more and more often
and in better roles.

Many of the stars remember their faithful fans
at Christmas and Easter and other occasions appropriate for greeting cards. They have special photographs taken in which they are posed in costumes
suitable to the seasons, holding lilies or bunnies or
holly berries or turkeys. Some of the masculine stars
are very gallant. Nelson Eddy sends Christmas
boxes of chocolates to the presidents of his fan
clubs in different cities. The fans for the singing
stars have a big advantage for they can buy their
star's records and listen to them over and over

again. That is the staple program of their meetings.

Now and then fan club presidents get a bit of publicity on their own. Marian Dommer, national president of the Joan Crawford Club, wrote such a good letter about *Mannequin's* being Joan's "most thrilling picture" that the New York papers carried an advertisement with a quotation and a picture at the top of Marian writing the letter. The Official Joan Crawford Club is probably the most elaborately organized of all the fan clubs. Their introductory letter, under a heading in Old English type, reads:

Dear Inquirer:

Thank you so much for your request for information about our organization. I shall be glad to tell you all about it, and I do hope that you will be interested.

The Official Joan Crawford Club was organized in September 1931 and is today one of the oldest and largest active clubs in existence. We have members in all sections of this country, as well as in many distant parts of the world, England, Ireland, Australia, Scotland, South Africa, and even Java included.

Miss Crawford takes a keen interest in all of our activities. Not only does she send personally autographed pictures to all of our new members, but she writes a long letter to the members for each edition of our club publication; and she also answers all your questions about her in "Joan's Question Box," a regular feature of the magazine.

We are really quite proud of our magazine, which includes many interesting articles about Miss Craw-

other means than the press. It sends out talent
scouts through the land, traveling sometimes un-
announced, sometimes with definite appointments,
so there is no leading man in any college play, no
winner of a local beauty contest who does not see
the glittering vision of a screen test. It has become
so much the thing for beauty contests, whether
organized by municipalities, factories, Rotary
Clubs, or newspapers, to send the winner on to
Hollywood that the studios have had to develop
a technique of discouragement. The applicant is
met at the gate of the company affiliated with the
contest, rushed through a routine tour of the lot,
given a screen test which is immediately checked,
is told she will not do, and bundled onto a plane
before she has had time to catch her breath or make
arrangements to stay on in the glamour city hoping
that her luck will change.

Even without the impetus of a beauty prize an
enormous number of hopefully dreaming young
women, and men, get themselves to Hollywood
urged on by the admiration of their friends or the
evidence of their own mirrors. They are urged frequently, too, by astrological predictions. The
power of the practitioners of the necromantic art
is spectacularly manifest in Hollywood.

The seekers for glamour live precariously, studying acting and singing, working in restaurants and
beauty parlors, taking care to look always as pretty

as possible in preparation for the great moment when some producer or other power notices them. So long has the immigration been going on that many of them have given up their dreams of fame for marriage and domesticity and are populating Southern California with a younger generation of surprising beauty.

The only really effective lion in the path of the screen-struck folk is the Central Casting Corporation. Central Casting, established in 1926, was invented by Mary van Kleeck of the Russell Sage Foundation when Mr. Hays invited her to go to Hollywood and give him some expert advice on how to handle most humanely the pitiful mobs besieging the studios for work. Unlike the private agencies it supplanted, Central Casting operates without fees. The Bureau speaks out plain in figures that should make an impression on anyone not completely giddy with her own charm. Perhaps those figures ought to be posted annually in all high schools, restaurants, department stores, and beauty parlors. There are plenty of girls who do not expect to leap overnight into stardom who are quite confident that they can get work as extras, and being an extra will do very well while you are waiting for your big chance. Extras after all are actors and they get ten dollars a day.

Central Casting's figures for 1938 are these. They must be read through.

Extras earned in 1938 . . $2,848,445.68
Total number of individuals
  used in 1938 . . . 8,875
Average days worked per in-
  dividual per year . . 29.77
Average daily wage . . $10.78
Average annual earnings per
  individual . . . $320.92
    6,850 earned less than $500

At the switchboard in the Bureau's office sit girls repeating, seventeen thousand times a day, the phrase that Central Casting has evolved as the briefest satisfactory answer to the inquiring extra: "Try later." "Try later." "Try later." It is the secondary theme in the music of glamour.

IV

CINEMA FASHIONS

WHEN Greta Garbo returned to America in the fall of 1934 she almost precipitated a national crisis. She wore her blonde hair cut so that it just cleared her shoulders, and it was perfectly straight. Every newspaper announced the appalling fact; every photograph showed it. The hairdressers were in despair. Garbo was for millions of women the ideal. Was there to be no more waved hair?

Fortunately, the hairdressers were equal to the occasion. They persuaded the American woman, the feminine portion of the eighty-five million, that only the Great Garbo could be really lovely with string straight hair; her emulators might approach the same effect by combing their hair—blonde hair if possible—straight down over their ears, and then curling under the ends of the long bob. The idea proved sound. The hairdressers were saved, and thousands of women with long curled-under bobs went about hoping that they reminded their friends of Great Garbo.

This Garbo situation was, according to the hair stylists associations, the second great influence of the movies on the American head. The first was Jean Harlow, when she appeared as a platinum blonde. That was in *Hell's Angels*, as long ago as 1930, but the hairdressing profession still remembers how women flocked to the beauty parlors asking to be made to look like that lovely girl with the shimmering hair. The press agent's phrase "platinum blonde" has gone into the language.

The third great influence was Norma Shearer's *Juliet*. She appeared in 1936, and for a year or two afterward almost every other girl in the country wore her hair smooth on the crown and curling up into a soft fluff below her ears. It was a pretty fashion, becoming to most people, following natural lines, youthful, not too difficult to care for, yet needing enough attention to keep the hairdressers in bread. According to the hair stylists Juliet's coiffure was Greek in origin, suggested by the Olympic games. Publicity stories reported that Norma Shearer borrowed it, with variations, from Gladys Swarthout. Adrian, designer for MGM, has put it on record that it was inspired by an angel head in Fra Angelico's "Annunciation." Whatever its origin it was Norma Shearer who presented it to the nation and she actually set two fashions at the same time for she added to the coiffure a little fifteenth-century headdress which became known as the Juliet cap and, made of anything from string to pearls, appeared all winter at every party in the country.

This double influence is a good example of the power of the movies to popularize a style wherever it may have originated. No fashion magazine, however skillfully edited, can compete with them when it comes to making it seem imperative to own a particular hat or frock or necklace. Neither adjectives nor photographs nor drawings can make a woman feel about an evening wrap as she feels when she sees it on the shoulders of Irene Dunne or in the arms of William Powell. It is both the glamorous background against which it was originally seen and the, probably unconscious, recollection of what was said to the lady wearing that high-collared velvet cape which makes it seem infinitely desirable when it is hanging on a clothes rack in the local dry goods emporium.

It is obvious enough today, but it took some years to convince the retailers of this magic force of the movies. The man who harnessed their power, much as Franklin harnessed lightning from the clouds, was Bernard Waldman of Modern Merchandising Bureau, Inc. Mr. Waldman is the originator and entrepreneur of Cinema Fashions, Screen Star Styles, Cinema Modes, and other glamorous trade names. It is his business to guess, while a film is still in production, which of the frocks, hats, or gadgets worn by the stars the average American woman is likely to take to her heart, provided she is given a very good chance.

Like the motion picture producer, Mr. Waldman has no illusions about influencing public taste; he merely tries to anticipate it. Offer the American woman, he will tell you, something too uncomfortable, impractical, or difficult to wear and, though it may be displayed and exploited by the loveliest of stars, she will turn away to purchase the, for her purposes, better garment worn by a comparatively unimportant bit player. If a fashion is good in itself, though, the fact that a big picture and a big star launch it will make it sweep the country.

Modern Merchandising works in coöperation with the designers in all the big studios who have no objection at all to creating for the screen with one eye upon the average American woman. Unhappily, though, for the average woman it can be only one eye. The designer must think first of the individuality of the player he is dressing and of the photographic qualities of stuffs and lines and colors. This does not prevent Mr. Waldman from seeing possibilities in forty or fifty pictures a year. He recognizes, for instance, the potentialities of the pirate costumes in *The Buccaneer* and he gets a New York manufacturer to turn out for him blouses called "The Boss," "The General," "Dominique." Tagged as Cinema Fashions they go into stores in cities from Bangor to Honolulu. Attached to each is a label with a pirate's head, cocked hat and long mustache, and the legend "A Buccaneer Fashion, inspired by *The Buccaneer*, a Paramount Picture." The women who flock to buy them never take the trouble to wonder how it came about that just when they are thinking how becoming those dashing pirate necklines or striped jerseys might be they walk into the local department store and find feminine adaptations of them on sale. Modern Merchandising restricts the supply of cinema fashions to one store in each city and from that store they get a commission on sales. At first the movie companies used to ask for 1 per cent of the profits. Now they are satisfied with the publicity. Cinema Fashions appear in the big cities but their strongest influence is in the small towns. There the movies have little else to compete with as the dictators of fashion.

Modern Merchandising began in 1930 when Mr. Waldman persuaded the firm for which he was then working to turn out duplicates of the golden-wedding dress they had created for Universal's *King of Jazz*. Everybody in the trade scoffed at the idea at first. They said the movies had no influence on fashion. The American public today is convinced that they have an influence on practically everything.

Cinema Fashions are only one means of spreading the influence of the stars. Individual manufacturers of every sort of apparel and accessory are constantly attending previews of important pictures and obtaining permission to reproduce this or that article of dress. Even Fifth Avenue shops find a motion picture name now and then to their advantage. Merle Oberon's *Wuthering Heights* wedding gown, for instance, graced one upper Fifth Avenue window while hats from the film were shown in another, and a reproduction of one of the rooms in a third. "Exclusive in this country," ran an advertisement in the *New York Times*, "Snow White afternoon dress. Scenes from Walt Disney's *Snow White and the Seven Dwarfs* which opens today at the Music Hall. Enchanted by their 'essentially Gallic spirit' Colcombet, fine French fabric house, secured exclusive rights. Every precious yard imported for dresses came straight to us. We've used it knowingly for piquant, conversation-making dresses. Silk crepe, a brilliant multicolor print on white or dark brown, $39.95." In the little towns they name anything they have in the shop after the movie of the week when an energetic theater manager suggests a "tie-up" to them in the right terms.

The stars' off-screen costumes are important too. Every fan magazine devotes pages to frocks modeled for it by this or that Hollywood beauty, topflight stars as well as those winging their way up. Sometimes the lady shows what she has selected from a rich collection as the "ideal date dress" or the perfect outfit for a winter cruise. Sometimes the camera has caught her off guard on the tennis court or at the Trocadero and the fashion editor fills up details with elaborate information about materials and cut. Sometimes it is merely a "type" dress, a Sonja Henie blouse at $2.98, "each with her own autograph on the label," or a series of "Judy Garland dresses that will give any young Miss the 'Swing and Smartness' of this famous MGM star." Or you might get from Wrigley's a pattern for the "Sonja Henie Double Mint gum dress adapted from her applause-getting Norwegian skating costume."

Yet another type of service is furnished by some of the more sophisticated fan magazines that keep reporters on the lots to tell you what the new pictures have to offer in fashion as well as in acting and plot. Their experts write learnedly in terms of trends and influences and designers, and even go so far now and then as to disapprove of some important star's costume in a big scene, a proceeding which gives their criticism a great flavor of authority.

Fashions in cosmetics the stars influence, of course, moving the trend towards heavy or light make-up, artificial or natural lines, and here they have, too, the power of endorsement. A movie queen famed for her lovely mouth is a better argument for buying a certain brand of lipstick than a society matron, however pedigreed, whom the customers have never seen.

Yet another way of fashion influence the movies have: they serve as a standard of reference, making it possible for the housewife in Vermont or Oregon to explain to her hairdresser, her dressmaker, or her decorator the ideal that she is striving to realize. "I want a sofa like the one in Bette Davis's drawing-room in *Dark Victory*." "Do you remember the collar Claudette Colbert wore in the picture last week? Well, I thought something like that on my black crêpe would make it look up-to-date." "I want my curls to go up on the side like Irene Dunne's in the dinner scene in *Love Affair*. Don't you think I'm enough her type to wear them that way?"

There enters here a still more insidious influence. Deep in the heart of woman after woman lies the conviction that she is the Claudette Colbert or the Carole Lombard or the Hedy Lamarr type. Sometimes subtly, sometimes very obviously she dresses herself accordingly. At times the results are happy. If she really has something of the outline or manner of her ideal she can get ideas for the magnification of her good points which might never occur to her unaided imagination. At times she goes astray in choosing her type, selecting what she would like to be rather than what she is, and the imitation is in consequence a trifle short of perfection.

There is something admirable as well as funny

in this striving after ideals. One of the powers of the pioneer is the belief in the possibility of improvement, the conviction that something more can be made of what you've got. The movies cater effectively to that deep-rooted instinct. An interesting example is the American exploitation of the English film *Pygmalion*. The publicity men mentioned the fact that it was written by George Bernard Shaw but what they stressed was that it showed the transformation of a flower seller into a duchess. The shop girls went to see how it was done. When the picture was running in Cleveland the Public Library circulated a list of "Books Eliza Should Have Read": *Well-Bred English, Look Your Best, Individuality and Clothes, Give Yourself Background*, and so on. Every one of them was in continuous circulation while the picture was in town.

It is not only the matron and the would-be glamour girl whose dress and appearance are influenced by the movies. With the increase in the number of juvenile stars it is possible for a young person of almost any age to find a model on the screen. Before she is old enough to copy the starry lady she hopes to look like when she grows up she can fashion herself on such youthful heroines as Judy Garland, Deanna Durbin, and the Lanes. If she is younger than that, she has always Shirley Temple. That powerful little person is an influence on her contemporaries both for good and ill. The

million dolls; four million cakes of Dwarf soap. There were pencil sets and hats and underwear and even hundred-dollar bracelets with dwarf charms. *Snow White* practically saved the toy business in the usually slack months after Christmas. The picture was responsible for two million dollars worth of toy sales. One factory making rubber dwarfs had to work twenty-four hours a day to fill orders.

By this tangible as well as visual influence the movies, together with radio and the comic strip, are building up a whole new American folklore. It is their creatures that our children want to hear stories about, to keep little models of on their desks, to have printed on their sweaters, to take to bed with them. The only real characters for whom they have anything like the same kind of affection are the heroes of the Western serials who share a good many of the cartoon characters' traits.

Two of the qualities which the cartoon characters must have are virtues which, as we saw in Chapter III, the fan thinks fundamental in a glamorous star: personality and energy. The cartoon characters are not required, however, to have glamour; they are seldom rich; and they are all of them exceedingly plain. Is personality a definitely American virtue? Have the folk heroes of other nations, the giants, the fairies, had individuality as Donald Duck has it or Popeye? Energy and the ability to win against odds have, of course, been

admired in all climes and ages. The cartoon characters go, in each film, through gargantuan difficulties but they always come out on top and the
virtues by which they win are the pioneer virtues—
courage, endurance, persistence, industry, quick
wit. Teachers College has given academic sanction
to this new and exemplary folklore by endorsing a
Mickey Mouse primer.

The educators have not yet put on record their
opinion of the work of the movies in destroying
folklore. A curious phenomenon of the 1938
Christmas was the substitution of the Lone Ranger
for Santa Claus. This was observable particularly
in the toy departments of stores in New York,
Brooklyn, and Chicago where the lure to the
young customer was not the opportunity to see
a live Santa Claus and whisper your Christmas
wishes in his ear but to "See the Lone Ranger's
helper at work at his forge, casting his silver bullets.
See 'Hi-yo, Silver! Away!'—our hero riding off in
a cloud of dust." No one was allowed to imper-
sonate the Ranger but the young were permitted
to gaze on huge statues of the masked cowboy
sitting easily on Silver who stood, as usual, on his
hind legs. In addition to this there were a few live
Indians and small mechanical tableaux showing
such popular adventures as the rescue by the
Ranger of a beautiful girl just as the stagecoach
topples off a cliff. It was also possible to have your
picture taken with the figure of the Lone Ranger.

The relation of all this to Christmas, except as Christmas is a good time to get someone to give you a Lone Ranger cowboy outfit, was not very clear but it is a development that will bear careful watching.

When it comes to the influence on children of the regular feature film parents and teachers are much less tranquil than they are about cartoons. In 1933 their uneasiness was crystallized by a book called alarmingly *Our Movie Made Children*. It was a popular summary of an elaborate investigation undertaken by the Payne Fund at the suggestion of the Motion Picture Research Council "to determine the influence of motion pictures on the public." By a variety of tests and experiments the investigators came to such conclusions as that motion pictures are a cause of delinquency and crime; that the pictures contain too much crime, love, and sex to make a wholesome diet for children; that the exhibition of gangster pictures in slum neighborhoods "amounts to the diffusion of poison"; that the conduct of screen characters is lower than the prevailing standards of morality; that children who go to the movies are likely to be less well behaved in school than the non-moviegoers; that moviegoing is highly detrimental to children's sleep; that moviegoing produces "profound mental and psychological effects of an emotional order."

Other writers had suggested such ideas before and plenty of parents had thought of them for themselves but to have them confirmed by "science" was alarming. The alarm spread from the parents to the industry. They felt it necessary to refute the Payne Fund studies. They found an ally in a book on *Art and Prudence* by Mortimer Adler, Professor of the Philosophy of Law at the University of Chicago. His study was concerned with the whole problem of art, morality, and censorship as related to the motion picture but much space was devoted in the course of his argument to exploding the pseudoscientific conclusions reached by the Payne Fund. Professor Adler made quite clear the inadequacy of the investigators' technique and the prejudiced nature of their conclusions but since his ponderous volume, which ranged from Aristotle to John Dewey, was far more than any distraught mother could be expected to cope with the industry induced Raymond Moley to make a brief summary, *Are We Movie Made?* He demonstrated the negative almost too well, not only blasting the Payne studies but disregarding considered opinions of teachers and other investigators which might have been of value. Undoubtedly the conclusion to which he and Adler came is, for the present at any rate, true: "On the crucial point—the influence of motion pictures on moral character and conduct—science has not improved or altered the state of existing opinion."

Existing opinion is easy to find if not to classify. It runs all the way from the individual fears of anxious mothers who wrote in distress to the Universal studios when it was announced that Deanna Durbin would elope in her next picture—and stopped the elopement, to the social questions raised by the Beards in their discussion of the movies in *America in Midpassage*. They are speaking of the opinion of the producers that what people most want to see is sex appeal.

An unusual feature . . . was the flaunting of sex before little boys and girls who crowded the moving-picture houses day and night. Though in countries accustomed to sex slavery, nautch girls, sing-song girls, and geisha girls learned to participate in sex entertainment in their early years, never before in America had boys and girls ranging from six to ten years of age been permitted by the millions to witness daily displays of sex enticements approaching, as near as censorship would permit, to the climax itself. Just what effect "a century of progress" in that kind of education would have upon the morale of human relations and upon the institution of the family no one could say with knowledge but, given the lust for motion-picture profits, joined to the passions of sex, that form of "progress" was certainly rapid.

The young people who go to these displays of sex enticement may not be aware of all the education they are getting but they do go to the movies, many of them, quite deliberately to learn social techniques. A favorite star can show even more authoritatively than an older sister, and much more explicitly, how to decline an invitation from a bore, how to accept a present, how to avoid and when to permit a kiss. There are minor social skills, too, taught more expertly by the movies than by the books of etiquette and studied carefully by young people of both sexes: how to light your friend's cigarette, how to walk with a girl, how to tip a waiter, how to deliver a wisecrack or a gallant speech. The Lynds' *Middletown* has an amusing documentary record of a drugstore conversation in which a high-school boy tries on one girl after another as they come in the most effective line in last night's movie. Any mother puzzled by the behavior of a youthful son or daughter would do well to study the star whose pictures they are most eager to see. She may find the explanation of some otherwise unaccountable actions.

The things the movies teach the young, and their elders too, may be a cause for amusement or a cause for alarm but some educators contend that the thing to worry about is not what the movies teach but what they leave out. Only by extreme regimentation, they say, can you be certain of fostering any idea in the youthful mind. The great service the movies can render is not to keep children away from sex and crime but to introduce them to truth. What is wrong with the movie universe is not its immorality but its narrowness. They believe that while the cinema in a totalitarian state is occupied in demonstrating and dramatizing the ideas the government thinks its people ought to hold, in showing them the way of life they ought to follow, it is the province of the cinema in a democratic country to open windows on a wider world. The American movie, they say, considering its opportunities, uses an absurdly limited number of windows. They like to tell the story of the affable potentate in Malay who greeted his first American visitor with the pleasant assurance: "We know all about the United States from your movies. Now which class of Americans do you belong to? Are you a gangster, a cowboy, or a crooner?"

The American child, of course, finds correctives for such impressions as soon as he leaves the theater but the story serves to show that the movies are letting one of their strongest powers rust unused. Why should they not, the educators ask, make their audiences familiar with a wide variety of ways of life? That the public is interested in the details of work, in the problems, the difficulties, and rewards of a profession of which they know little at first hand should stand proved, it would seem, to the industry by the doctor cycle. The screen has shown doctors operating in the most spectacularly equipped of theaters, and with makeshift instruments in a country kitchen. The family practitioner has been pictured, the interne, the ambulance surgeon, the psychiatrist—serious and burlesque—the research man in his laboratory. The eighty-five million look and ask for more. The doctor has been dramatized and romanticized, granted, but there is much truth in the medical pictures too. The educators want to see the same combination of exact exposition and legitimate romanticizing tried on other professions. It has been done with the army and the navy, they point out; why not with some of the skilled and daring mechanical trades in which so many Americans are engaged? Engineering has been barely suggested on the screen; mining shown only in moments of disaster; our innumerable and fascinating manufacturing occupations scarcely touched at all.

The industry sighs and points to the trouble it gets into whenever it departs from the gangster, crooner, cowboy formula. They declare that the only hero, and likewise villain, who never gets them into difficulties is American, white, and unemployed. If they step out of those bounds they fall foul of some racial or national group or some one of the professions. The *Journal of the American Bar Association*, to be sure, thinks well of the movies. The editors made a study of the treatment of lawyers on the screen during the last six months of 1938 and found that seven out of eight judges in major roles and twenty out of twenty-four in minor roles had been sympathetically portrayed. In only one out of twenty-eight instances was there "an unsympathetic portrayal of a lawyer without a contrasting lawyer appearing as a sympathetic character." The Butlers Club of America has elected to honorary presidency the actor Arthur Treacher, nationally known as the perfect butler of the screen, but these are bright exceptions. The Citizens Chiropractic Committee of the American Bureau of Chiropractic sued Alan Mowbray when he played, in *There Goes My Heart*, a street car motorman who was taking a night correspondence course in chiropractic. Chiropractic, they said, requires four full years of study. Newspaper men, who have more opportunity than most workers to express their views in print, are continually taking issue with the movie portraits of reporters although, as Douglas Churchill of the *New York Times* put it, "the cinematic conception of news men as gay irresponsible fellows who live hard and only for today, probably has been responsible for more young men entering the craft than all the schools of journalism in America." The Hays office has been upset enough by the newspaper men's banter to order a reform. Joseph Breen, administrator of the Production Code, wrote to Hal Roach when he had examined the script of *The Housekeeper's Daughter:*

Suggested in your script is a very important question of industry policy. This comes about by way of the characterization of newspaper men as drunkards who go about "cadging" drinks and generally conducting themselves in a thoroughly offensive and unethical manner. Such characterization is certain to give offense to newspaper publishers, editors and writers, and, because of this, the characterization should be entirely changed.

Commenting on individual scenes he added: "There should be no suggestion that the newspaper men are chiseling Veroni out of payment for their drinks," and "We think it better that you eliminate the line, 'A city editor, like a pun, is the lowest form of wit.'"

The industry offers this as one more instance that it is not imposing stereotypes upon its audience but trying with all its might to reproduce their ideas. They can cite as many examples of this as you please. There are, for instance, the requirements set down by youthful moviegoers for their cowboy heroes. Dick Foran once explained them in an instructive interview:

You can be respectful, devoted, even pally with the heroine, but you can't do any tender love scenes, because if you do, you're apt to get hoots and cat-calls. Then, the hero has always got to be good to his horse, and the horse has to be as dolled up as the hero; the hero may wound the villain, but never kill him. Villain may plunge over a cliff, but hero's hands must be clean of suspicion of murder. If the hero and villain shoot it out, the hero has to give the villain a break on the draw. And the hero must never miss with a gun, once he's drawn it. Every picture has to point a moral, and it's considered good business to have your horse save you at least once in every Western. Hero can go into a saloon and order a drink, but he must never really down it.

The industry cites also the decision to abandon the *Mr. Moto* series of detective stories because anti-Japanese feeling is running so high in America that audiences can no longer take pleasure in the courage and astuteness of a member of that nation.

Then there is the case of the screen negro. The eighty-five million are primarily white and no white American, the industry maintains, would ever make his escape personality black. "Stardom," Terry Ramsaye wrote in the *Motion Picture Herald* (July 8, 1939) is

a job of vicarious attainment for the customers. The starring player becomes the agent-in-adventure for the box-office customer. The spectator tends to identify himself with the glamorous and triumphant player, just as the tense, weakling little ribbon clerk in the last rim of seats clenches his fists and wins with the winner at the prize fight. . . .

Inevitably the motion picture tends to place the negro in the screen drama in the same relation as that which he occupies in the nation's social and economic picture. In other words the screen public takes the negro as the average of 135,000,000 takes him.

The fact that the negro is better accepted on his merits as an artist by the stage is but another of the endless and obvious evidences of the devotion of the stage to minorities of more sophistication, more erudition, more capacity for intellectual adventure.

The multitude can chuckle at Step'n Fetchit and laugh with Rochester, but they will woo and win with the Gables, the Taylors and the Coopers. That's "the major responsibility"—the white actor's burden.

The producer is ready to protect the negro and avoid stirring race hatreds by keeping off the modern screen such villainous negroes as appeared in Griffith's *Birth of a Nation*, but the best he thinks he can do beyond that is to make the negro so amusing and agreeable that an audience is always pleased at the appearance of a black face. A negro may also appear in a position where he excites not laughter but sympathy. The negro janitor suspected of the murder in *They Won't Forget* is the best example of this class. He is probably the most realistic negro, thanks to the script but also to remarkably fine acting, that the screen has seen. The all-negro *Green Pastures*, for all its originality and, at some points, elevation, permitted a certain feeling of superiority on the part of the audience.

To prove to Hollywood that its gauges of audience reaction may be inaccurate a project is now under way for the production of all negro films. The Greater New York Committee for Better Negro Films has been organized to make, through the agency of that skillful and courageous experimental group Frontier Films, true pictures about the negro.

The educators of the young see in such movements a light of hope. They see another in a recent development in the commercial film, the steadily increasing popularity of the family picture which has now definitely reached the proportions of a cycle. It is not easy, as it is in some cases, to put a finger on the big successful picture that started it all. The trend began probably when the Hardy series, conceived by their producer as sound B pictures, moved into A esteem on a mounting wave of critical approval and public enthusiasm. The Hardy pictures are based on research as intelligent and thorough as that which goes into the making of the most elaborate "historical." What is the size of the typical American family? Five—father, mother, son, daughter, and one other relative; the Hardy creators made it a youngish aunt. What is the typical family's income? How large a house do they have? How much domestic help do they employ? Do they own a car? How much do they travel? Have they ever been to the opera? Questions like that were carefully considered and answered to the satisfaction, it would seem, of the eighty-five million. The things that happen to the Hardys are the sort of things that might happen to almost anyone and their responses to the various situations are both entertaining and accurate. Because they are so genuine an American norm, families in the various brackets far above or below them see themselves also mirrored in the Hardys.

The careful research done for the family pictures has effected, to begin with, a refreshing reform in motion picture interior decoration. Why an industry which expends endless pains to find the exact dimensions of the Czar's palace in 1811 or the precise kind of rocking chair used by Mark Twain's aunt never bothered to examine the interior of an ordinary middle-class home was long a puzzle. Before the Hardys came family dwellings were furnished, apparently, by men who had lived so long in Hollywood that they had forgotten about the rest of America. The producers were aware what they were doing when they improved upon the proportions of Norma Shearer's Versailles but they seemed unconscious that they were exaggerating in the same proportions the abode of every American in modest circumstances. The exaggeration was applied to the small-town family and also to the penniless working girl in the big city. She had always in her hall bedroom a chaise longue, a tea table, a stream-lined bridge lamp, and an electric kitchenette. The working girls still live in luxury, though there was one real rooming-house bedroom in *Stage Door*, but the Hardys' house, inside and out, and their town of Carvel, are cheeringly familiar. So are the houses of the other screen families, the Joneses who are not quite so widely acquainted as the Hardys but well liked and of longer standing and the other serial families who are now being born.

The same intelligent realism is present in a steadily increasing succession of pictures with

Decorators and furniture dealers reproduced for their clients the rooms which they admired in "Dark Victory."

The Hardys at breakfast. There is a growing enthusiasm for pictures of average American families in realistic settings.

Production on location: "Union Pacific" extras and crew sit down to lunch.
Production in the studio: Henry M. King directing "Stanley and Livingstone" in an African jungle on the Twentieth Century-Fox lot.

V

THE INDUSTRY

I T must be remembered that the production of motion pictures is not only an art but an industry." Or: "It must be remembered that the production of motion pitures is not so much an art as an industry." Or: "It must be remembered that the production of motion pictures is not an art but an industry." That sentence, in one of its variants, occurs in every discussion of the movies. When you know how any given writer uses it you can predict most of his other opinions about the screen.

The Hays office compromises and speaks of the "art-industry." Certainly with the movie, more even than with the theater or the book, the industry is essential to the art. Without the triple industrial structure of production, distribution, and exhibition the art of the motion picture could not exist at all.

PRODUCTION

THE producers spend much money and ingenuity in reminding theater managers of "the consistently high quality of RKO pictures" or "the large number of ranking box-office stars on the roles of MGM"; they do very little to assist the general public to distinguish between one motion picture company and another. The theater man buys his product on the strength of the company's promises and past performance; the moviegoer buys his, a single picture at a time, on the strength of the advertising or the story or the stars. When they address the eighty-five million the producers talk chiefly about the greatness of a picture's theme or the glamorous qualities of the actors who interpret it. Occasionally they mention a director, a composer, or a script writer. About themselves they say little, yet, so often are they seen on screen and poster and newspaper page, the names of the major producing companies, the Big Eight, are household words. Columbia, Metro-Goldwyn-Mayer, Paramount, RKO-Radio, Twentieth Century-Fox, Universal, United Artists, Warner Brothers; every school child knows that those are motion picture companies. Mention one of the smaller concerns, an independent producer, a maker of "shorts" or "quickies," and you will find that only the cinematically erudite have any idea who he is.

The producers, large and small, are not concerned about this. They work competitively in exploiting their individual movies but they work coöperatively in presenting "the industry" to the public; "Motion Pictures Are Your Best Entertainment." The details of the production job they have no particular desire to communicate to the layman. There is a certain feeling that information about trade practices tends to dim glamour. When the producers talk about production it is in large generalities and frequently in terms of dollars. The chief thing that the eighty-five million know, or think they know, about movie production is that it is fabulously and recklessly expensive. The companies cater wholeheartedly to the general American impression that if a thing costs enough it must be good. They have talked so often of million-dollar productions that they are now obliged, when they want to make an impression, to talk of two millions or three. What the million or the two millions involve, besides large salaries to the stars, the average citizen knows only vaguely. He probably cannot tell you how little it costs to make a "quickie." These facts are no secrets but they are to be found chiefly in the trade publications of the industry. In the *International Motion Picture Almanac*, for instance, there is a typical budget for a million-dollar picture:

Cast	$250,000
Extras, bits, characters	50,000
Director	100,000
Director assistants	20,000
Cameraman and crew	15,000
Lights	20,000
Make-up, hairdressers, supplies . . .	9,000
Teachers	2,000
Crew and labor	12,000
Story preparation	70,000
Story costs	50,000
Costumes and designers	20,000
Sets and art directors	125,000
Stills and photographs	4,000
Cutters	10,000
Film negative	10,000
Tests	12,000
Insurance	20,000
Sound engineering and negatives . .	31,000
Publicity, transportation, research, technical, miscellaneous	20,000
Indirect costs	150,000
Total	$1,000,000

That table gives one a fair idea of the division
of costs in any high-priced feature picture. If it has
a reasonable success it should cover expenses and
make a profit of several hundred thousand. A "B"
or "program picture," one good enough to serve
as second feature on a double bill, can be made for
from $75,000 to $100,000. A "quickie" can be
turned out for as little as $10,000. A "quickie" is
one of those Westerns or action melodramas that
the small movie house shows as its second feature.

It is made in less than a week, by an independent producer who rents space in one of the big studios after he has his staff, his cast, and his story all lined up and ready to go.

With sordid production facts of this kind the eighty-five million trouble themselves very little. They are content to drink down their glamour and excitement and escape without questioning the sources or the initial cost. The fans generally confine their enthusiasm and curiosity to researches in the minutiae of the lives of the stars. But there is a steadily increasing number of people who are interested in the way movies are made and want to know more about it. For them publicity men tell production stories and newspapers print them. There is much production information, too, in the fan magazines, though the emphasis there is almost entirely on actors and acting. Occasionally a movie like *A Star Is Born* or *Stand-In* shows the fascinated spectator some of the things that go on on a Hollywood lot. Books about the film, serious books most of them, are steadily increasing; books on the history of the motion picture, on camera problems, on directoral technique, biographies of actors and producers, critical discussions of the cinema as art. There are serious film magazines too.

Much of the public incentive to read and learn has come from the Better Film Councils. They have worked on the logical assumption that the more an audience knows about the problems of technique the better equipped it is to understand and appreciate an art. They have tried to make their constituencies, whether they are women's clubs or school children, curious about the way movies are made.

A popular device with the Better Film lecturer is to recall to his listeners a sequence in some recent movie, say a holdup scene in one of the big spectacular Westerns. He describes what the audience saw on the screen and then he shows how many hours of thought and care, how much expert knowledge and technical skill went to the making of those brief exciting minutes. He tells how a research department studied the period in detail; how a property department constructed a minutely perfect stagecoach, guns, bows, arrows; how a costume department concerned itself not only with authenticity and design and fit but with the photogenic qualities of materials; how make-up men work; how horses can fall without killing their riders or offending the SPCA; how scenes are planned and set and lighted; how actors are rehearsed; how sound and music are synchronized with the picture.

The emphasis falls in these talks almost invariably on just those points in which the American film excels. So much ingenuity, skill, cash, and genius are annually expended in the perfection of technical methods and devices that there is now practically nothing the American movie cannot say if it wants to; with the question of what it should want to say the Better Film lecturers concern themselves less.

It is good for any art to have an audience which is aware, even superficially, of the kind of problems that must be met and solved. It is still better for an art to have an audience which has tried its own hand at the solutions. The mechanically minded young American of today is almost instinctively interested in camera work and lighting and sound reproduction. He takes to them as he takes to cars and radios. He not only wants to understand what the experts in Hollywood are doing; he wants to try experiments for himself. He wants to make his own movies. The number of film clubs in our high schools is legion and a large proportion of them is engaged not merely in studying professionally made films but in making their own movies of school life or local history or current events. Boys and girls both are fascinated by the problems of photography, of costume, of property and setting. There are some opportunities for acting, of course, which feed the romantic longing to get to Hollywood, but the majority of film club films are documentaries without stellar roles. There is not too much sidetracking of interest onto mere excitement and glamour. A great many individual Americans make movies, too, movies that range all the way from personal records made by a casually turned camera to elaborately planned and cut films.

These educated audiences are valuable to the movies far beyond the rest of the eighty-five million but they know really less about pictures than they think they do. The points on which they are least informed are precisely those in which the American motion picture is weakest. The film club member is very learned about "spots" and "cans" and "decibels" and "camera angles"; he does not know so much about what makes a good movie story and how a movie story should be told. The fundamental importance of the motion picture director is just beginning to dawn upon the American public.

The names of directors, to be sure, appear, all by themselves in large letters, on the screen but how many moviegoers who can tell you the name of every star and supporting player in any picture they have just seen have any idea who directed it? The actors have faces that can be recognized; they have concrete personalities. The directors have only creative personalities, a much more subtle and difficult thing to grasp. Suggest to a devoted fan that half the excellence of an actor's work in a particular picture might be credited to the director and he will feel that you have uttered blasphemy.

A mild campaign is now being made by the production companies in the directors' behalf. Movie advertising contains more and more frequently the announcement that a forthcoming colossal picture is the work of "that great director who gave you—" Previews of coming attractions occasionally show photographs of the director at work, ascending on a beam with a mounting camera or leaning forward intently in his special folding chair. Columbia Pictures actually took for the "keynote" of its 1939–40 sales campaign, not "great stories" or "great stars" but "great directors."

These are hopeful signs on the production horizon. The director has seldom had in Hollywood either the prestige he deserves or the power he requires. Fortunately the directors themselves are becoming increasingly militant. Organized in 1936, the Screen Directors Guild has just succeeded in getting itself recognized by the producers. In the summer of 1938 they published an analysis of the motion picture industry. It had become at that time a popular pastime to ask, What's wrong with the movies? and the directors thought themselves more qualified than most to give an answer:

It is the firm conviction of the Directors Guild that rehabilitation lies first in changing the present "system of production" which pervades the industry—namely, eliminating the involved, complicated, and expensive system of supervision which separates the director and writer from the responsible executive producers; . . .

No director questions the need of executive supervision, nor . . . the contribution of many individual producers who have given prodigiously to the industry. . . . We speak here of the army of the inept, who have been promoted to positions of authority for which they are unqualified, inexperienced, and utterly lacking in creative ability. A survey of the major studios has revealed that 40 per cent of the cost of production is represented by overhead and miscellaneous. Never in the history of the industry has this cost been so high. . . .

Even within the other 60 per cent is to be found a record of uncertainty, duplication, and waste . . .

In recent years most studios have faced an ever-increasing difficulty in meeting their release dates, and have fallen short of making the number of pictures yearly contracted for. This, in spite of the increasing number of producers and associate producers. In large measure this can be attributed directly to the growing estrangement between the producer and the director on the one hand, and the director and the writer on the other.

Let us be factual for a moment! Following is a brief summary of findings covering the position of the director today—in comparison to ten years ago. The most alarming and significant fact uncovered was the amazing increase in the producer class during the decade.

	1926-1927	*1936-1937*
Directors with feature credits	246	234
Producers including supervisors and associates . . .	34	220
	1927	*1937*
Feature American-made releases	743	484

Eight hundred per cent more producers to produce 40 per cent less pictures! . . .

The best pictures made in the industry are largely those in which the director has had real participation in their dramatic and mechanical structure from inception, in direct association with the executive producers without the interference of intermediaries. The success of this practice has had no weight in the industry—on the contrary the practice of developing this approach to pictures is on the wane—and many directors who, until recently, were offered creative opportunities are finding the doors progressively closed to them. . . .

What built the motion picture was "individuality." Freshness of approach, the unique touch which gives vivid experience. These were the creative elements which raised the nickelodeon to the motion picture industry. This individuality was largely the contribution of directors and writers. This may be disputed *ad infinitum* but it remains a fact that it is not material alone which is important to motion pictures but also the manner in which that material is registered on film in this infinitely imaginative and limitless medium. Today the system offers a virtual proscription against originality and freshness in pictures. This costs the industry millions of dollars.

To meet this dangerous state in our industry, the Directors Guild earnestly recommends that closer unity be established and maintained between the real producer on the one hand and the director and writer on the other, and that the directors bend every effort toward the re-establishment of the collaborative system which was, and still is, the money-making and good-picture-making fact of the past.

Even plainer terms than these were used by Frank Capra, President of the Guild. He is one of the few directors whose name the average moviegoer knows because he made those enormous successes *Mr. Deeds Goes to Town, It Happened One Night,* and *You Can't Take It with You.* In a letter to the *New York Times* (published April 2, 1939) Mr. Capra said:

There are only half a dozen directors in Hollywood who are allowed to shoot as they please and who have any supervision over their editing.

We all agree with you when you say that motion pictures are the director's medium. That is exactly what it is, or should be. We have tried for three years to establish a Directors Guild, and the only demands we have made on the producers as a Guild were to have two weeks' preparation for "A" pictures, one week preparation time for "B" pictures, and to have supervision of just the first rough cut of the picture.

You would think that in any medium that was the director's medium the director would naturally be conceded these two very minor points. We have only asked that the director be allowed to read the script he is going to do and to assemble the film in its first rough form for presentation to the head of the studio. It has taken three years of constant battling to achieve any part of this.

We are now in the process of closing a deal between director and producer which allows us the minimum of preparation time but still does not give us the right to assemble our pictures in rough form, but merely to assemble our sequences as the picture goes along. This is to be done in our own time, meaning, of course, nights and Sundays, and no say whatever in the final process of editing.

I would say that 80 per cent of the directors today shoot scenes exactly as they are told to shoot them without any changes whatsoever, and that 90 per cent of them have no voice in the story or in the editing. Truly a sad situation for a medium that is supposed to be the director's medium.

All of us realize that situation and some of us are trying to do something about it by insisting upon producer-director set-ups, but we don't get any too much encouragement along this line. Our only hope is that the success of these producer-director set-ups will give others the guts to insist upon doing likewise.

In February, 1939, Mr. Capra did something more about it. He threatened a strike of all the directors in Hollywood. That did the work. The Associated Motion Picture Producers recognized the Directors Guild as a bargaining agency and appointed a committee to draw up terms. The directors succeeded in establishing that for preparation prior to photography each director be allowed:

For pictures of over $2,000,000, two weeks,
For pictures of that amount or below, one week,
For Westerns and serials, five days,
For shorts, two days.

A strong indication that the directors have discovered the fundamental thing that is wrong with the movies is the enormous success of the pictures in which they have functioned, at least partially, as they want to function. Frank Capra chooses his own stories, edits and cuts his own films. He is credited with twenty-eight pictures, only one of which was not a commercial success. They are pictures which the eighty-five million went to see and still remember and which critics cite when they want to show you what they mean by a good movie. *Lost Horizon* was the ranking box-office success of 1937. *It Happened One Night* won the Motion Picture Academy Award for the best directed film of 1934; *Mr. Deeds Goes to Town* won it in 1936; *You Can't Take It with You* won it in 1938. Leo McCarey for *The Awful Truth* and *Love Affair* was producer, director, and collaborator on the script. *The Awful Truth* won the Academy award for 1937. John Ford worked in the same way on *The Informer*, *Stagecoach*, *Young Mr. Lincoln*. *The Informer* has become one of the classics of the screen. And these are not the only instances.

The directors' purpose in their fight for recognition of their Guild was not only artistic but social. They are concerned with the working conditions of the lower ranks of their profession, first and second assistant directors and unit managers. The agreement arranged for minimum salaries, hours of work, vacations with pay, and such matters.

In this action the directors have followed the

pattern of the other motion picture labor organizations, the Screen Writers Guild, the Screen Actors Guild, and the various technical unions, of which there are forty or more, most of them affiliated with the International Alliance of Theatrical and Stage Employees. The Screen Actors have concerned themselves with the wages and working hours of extras, and so on down the list.

It was only a few years ago that Hollywood began to be socially conscious. The swing may have been started by the socially minded dramatists and story writers whom the producers were importing in increasing numbers because their work was more and more interesting the public. It may have been the Spanish War, which roused eager partisanship for the anti-Fascist cause. Stars gave benefit parties; screen writers spoke at meetings; directors raised money for ambulances. Their interest spread from the oppressed in Europe to the oppressed in California. They worked for Tom Mooney. They helped the Salinas strikers. Then it began to seem to them important that working conditions in Hollywood should be tolerable to everybody. Agitation, organization, and action became the order of the day. Writers who used to complain that they drew salaries week after week with nothing to do became so busy that they could scarcely find time to attend a cocktail party unless it were for a cause. Rooms that had rung with gossip now rang with propaganda and debate and strategy. People who

had been away from Hollywood for six months
or more came back to find an almost unbelievable
change. They talked of it either with amusement
or excitement. The Dies Committee began to
worry about "radicalism" and "Communism" in
the major studios.

To most of the eighty-five million moviegoers
strike and union are words that have no connection at all with pictures. Nevertheless the eighty-
five million are going to be vitally affected by
Hollywood's changing point of view. If the people
who make the movies, the writers and directors
and actors, are interested in social problems they
are going to be interested from time to time in
making pictures that deal with social problems;
they will now and then inject an idea into a film
even if it started out without one, for the film
workers are beginning to see the relation of their
own problems to the whole labor movement and
the social scene. The Screen Writers Guild considers affiliation with the AFL or the CIO; actors
talk of the possibility of "one big union" which
would include artists of stage, screen, radio, and
television. The chief thing that now marks off the
movie artist or technician from other workers is
that, even though his work is exacting and his
hours long, he usually makes a pretty comfortable
living. Compared to the Detroit mechanic or the
migratory farm workers, the moving picture em-
ployee is a privileged individual. He has come into

the labor movement not through desperation but through thought, a fact which may have its importance for the future of the labor movement and the future of the screen.

The producers are at present the forces of reaction both in respect to labor conditions in the studios and to social themes in pictures. As soon as it becomes clear, though, through the box-office, that a large section of the eighty-five million want ideas as part of their entertainment the producers will begin to look for ideas—and will have no difficulty at all in finding artists of every rank who are full of them.

DISTRIBUTION

OF the distribution side of the motion picture business the general public knows practically nothing except two phrases: "block booking" and "blind buying." There is a sinister ring in the alliteration which adds to the general vague impression that they are nefarious practices. Just how wicked they appear on closer examination depends, of course, upon whom you ask. The big producers maintain that they could not do business efficiently on any other basis. Some exhibitors see in a modification of block booking their only chance of survival. The Motion Picture Research Council and the various women's organizations it has enlisted in its crusade believe that the elimination of block booking and blind buying would make the movies moral. What the truth of the matter is the Federal Government is now trying to decide.

The Government is approaching the problem from two directions: a suit on charges of monopoly in restraint of trade brought by the Department of Justice against the major production companies, and an investigation by the Department of Commerce, a sort of mutual benefit affair designed to clarify issues. The suit is of course by far the more important. Announced in the summer of 1938, it will probably be brought to trial in the winter of 1940 and will certainly not end until it has reached the Supreme Court.

The Government maintains that the fundamental necessity for the motion picture industry is the complete separation—"divorcement"—of exhibition and production. The major companies, they say, which own large chains of theaters sell their product to those chains at favorable rates and under favorable conditions. They sell at the same favorable rates to theaters belonging to the other major companies, while they discriminate against the independently owned theaters to such an extent that it is difficult for the independent exhibitor to buy films at profitable prices and often to exist at all. The majors have, the Government charges, divided the country among them so that the West Coast theaters, for instance, are chiefly owned by Fox, those in New England and the South by Para-

but on the public's interest in the making of news-reels, which was the basis of the plot.

Interesting and skillfully planned as this part of the business is, with its schedules, transportation, fire prevention devices, and departments for the repair of films, it is only a minor section of the distributor's main function, which is that of a sales-man. It is he who imposes blind buying and block booking.

Blind buying means simply that the exhibitor buys a film before he sees it, usually before it is made. The motion picture season runs, like the academic year, from September to September. In June or July the companies present their schedules for the months to come. Each of the majors pro-duces annually about fifty feature films, with a varied number of shorts, cartoons, and newsreels. The expenditure on the features is large, anywhere from a hundred thousand dollars to several mil-lions. The methods of financing are beyond the layman's vision but the producers feel the need to reckon returns by a pretty early date even though they never collect from an exhibitor until a film has actually been played. This, chiefly, be-cause many rentals are calculated on a percentage of the take at the box-office. In a business of such mammoth proportions, also, it is necessary for play-ing schedules, advertising, and exploitation activi-ties to be planned far in advance. The exhibitor has to be sure in September that he will have a picture in his house every evening next May.

What the producer has for sale, then, is a title, a star, and an outline. The exhibitor makes his selection on the basis of the enthusiasm in his neighborhood for certain glamorous names, the local popularity of a best seller, the marvels revealed by the press book about a new personality or plot, the amount of backing the company is giving the film in national advertising, and his faith in the producer's reputation for delivering the goods in the past.

This, according to some of the reformers of the movies, is not enough. The Neely Bill, which has passed the Senate but is not likely soon to come before the House, requires the producer to furnish the exhibitor with a detailed synopsis of each film he buys and makes any departure from that synopsis in the shooting of the picture a criminal offense. This looks to be an intolerable limitation of art, like forbidding a writer to make any changes while his book is in proof or a painter to alter a detail in a contract mural. Nor does it appear very clear how such a regulation would help the exhibitor to protect his community's morals. Of the Neely Bill and its supporters later. Suffice it here to say that the Government suit includes among its complaints nothing about blind buying.

Another possible alternative to blind buying is the practice in use in England where the film must be screened for the exhibitor before he purchases it. He is not, however, compelled to watch the screening and usually he doesn't. The American producer is delighted to give trade showings of his films and occasionally does but in a country which turns out five hundred feature films a year and includes in each of its distribution districts some hundreds of square miles how is the individual exhibitor to find time to see the available product and make his choice?

The method of selling in lots, block booking, is simply a wholesale selling practice. Of the fifty feature films each producer makes in a year some are practically certain to be good, at least by box-office standards; some are practically certain to be "flops"; others, in between. The major producer contends that if he makes a smaller number of films his equipment lies idle too much of the time and he must reckon a larger overhead on the films he does make. He contends also that unless he can sell his product in wholesale quantities he must charge so much for each picture that the exhibitor will not be able to afford it, or will be obliged to increase his admission costs. The movies will then, say the producers ominously, cease to be the art of the people.

The variation in the prices at which the same film is rented, or "sold," is enormous. It depends on theater size, conditions in the locality, and, very important, age. The prevalent American feeling that newness is a valuable quality in a work of art makes the first run of a film far more important commercially than it is in fact. Just as the general reader wants to be conversant with the news of the day, the man of the hour, or the book of the month, so the eighty-five million want instinctively to see the picture of the week. Some pictures, to be sure, are cut to topics of temporary interest which would fail to rouse any curiosity after six months' time; some derive what value they have from the fact that they are vehicles for a star at the zenith of his power; but in general a good story well told is a good story well told today or five years hence. It is a trifle fantastic, but certainly not entirely the fault of the industry, that a picture which commands a rental of $25,000 a week at a first run metropolitan house can be had a few weeks later by a small-town exhibitor for $10. The industry, as a matter of fact, delights to boast that when you buy its films "second-hand," for fifteen cents at a "subsequent run" house on a side street, you are getting, not a worn-out product, as you would in a transaction with any other manufacturer but an article of just as fine quality as that for which first-nighters paid $2.20 on Broadway.

The exhibitor who owns the only theater in a town can pretty well set his own prices and buy what films he likes from whom he likes. When two or more theaters are running in opposition, everybody begins to bargain. The exhibitor who pays for the first run of a film must insist that no one in his territory shall show it for a fairly long time afterwards, otherwise some of his potential audience will wait until they can see it for a quarter instead of forty cents. This protection of the first-run exhibitor is called "clearance," a trade practice accepted in principle but much disputed in operation. The exhibitor who buys thirty films from a distributor gets them at a better price than his rival who takes only two or three. This wholesale buying and selling constitutes block booking.

The usual practice is to offer the exhibitor a block of twenty or thirty or fifty films. Because he wants five of them very much and because he must have, say, thirty films of some kind anyway to keep his house open, the exhibitor takes the lot. Sometimes a block includes shorts and newreels, sometimes only features. The Government makes a distinction between selective block booking, by which the exhibitor is permitted to choose the films in his block, and compulsory block booking, by which he must take the block the distributor arranges. The independent theaters, the Government says, are frequently forced to take all or nothing. They are discriminated against also in the arrangement of playing dates. They are sometimes even told what admission price they must charge.

Block booking, then, is an evil only when it is practiced by a monopoly but, though it is actually an economic issue, it has been presented to the public as a question of community morals. Before they saw the prospect of relief through the Department of Justice many independent exhibitors had tried to get relief through state legislatures and through Congress, enlisting in their crusade the support of various community organizations. The result was a clouding of the real issue which has been clouded still further by the voluminous testimony presented by both sides in the Senate hearings on the Neely Bill and its predecessors. While the bill was before the Senate the producers were able to present convincing evidence that exhibitors are permitted, under the block-booking system, a wide privilege of cancellation and that they invariably use it to eliminate pictures they think will be bad box-office, not those that are "socially undesirable."

The real issue, as the Government has made clear, is far wider than a question of exhibitor taste; compulsory block booking is simply one discriminatory practice resulting from the ownership of theaters by producers or the ownership of production companies by theaters. The control of the major companies, the Government contends, constitutes a monopoly in restraint of trade, restricts freedom of community choice in films, and prevents the introduction of new ideas in production.

The whole monopoly question is obviously too complex for any one less well informed than the Government intends to be to settle. Whatever the outcome of the suit, and the industry, considering the present temper of the Supreme Court, does not approach it with optimism, the eighty-five million moviegoers will probably not feel any immediate effect. In the future, however, as now, the business structure of the motion picture industry will vitally influence the art of the motion picture.

The industry's first response to the monopoly suit was the launching of a great campaign to prove to the eighty-five million, and all the other Americans, that "Motion Pictures Are Your Best Entertainment." They did not say, of course, that it is pleasant to have plenty of friends around you when you meet the Government in court. Nor did they say, except to each other, that the eighty-five million attendance was declining rather than mounting and something must be done about it.

Motion Picture's Greatest Year began with fanfares. Producers, distributors, and exhibitors worked shoulder to shoulder. Governors issued proclamations; Chambers of Commerce coöperated; editorial writers pronounced benedictions. The central feature of the celebration was a movie quiz in which questions had to be answered on thirty out of some ninety-odd pictures and a brief essay written on which one you liked best. The prizes were of proper Hollywood size: fifty thousand dollars for the first, others ranging from twenty-five thousand dollars to ten. There was a small national flurry of excitement but the public proved singularly apathetic. The millions of answers expected materialized actually as a little over two and the prizes were finally awarded with comparatively little attention from the press. What the public evidently wanted, as the critics took pains to point out, was not better prizes or better slogans but better movies. Will Hays, in his annual report to the Motion Picture Producers and Distributors covered the great campaign in one brief paragraph:

The campaign in the summer of 1938 for greater theater attendance during the Fall season proved a splendid example of coöperation among all elements in the industry. Producers, distributors, and exhibitors met on a common platform of industry promotion to center attention on the better pictures of the season, recognizing that it was the common denominator of better entertainment that drew people to the theaters. It received full newspaper and trade press support.

Cinema's Golden Jubilee, the fiftieth anniversary of the shooting of the first scene by a movie camera, which was scheduled for celebration in the fall of 1939, was observed with considerable restraint.

A more secure and skillful shelter against the coming storm the industry has devised by writing a trade-practices code, an instrument, to use its favorite phrase, of "self-regulation" like the Production Code administered by the Hays office.

EXHIBITION

With the manager of his local theater the average moviegoer has his only personal contact with the industry. The state of mind in which each of the eighty-five million sees a movie is very largely a result of that exhibitor's conditioning. He takes, as we saw in Chapter II, a great deal of trouble to make his patrons feel that sitting in his theater is far pleasanter than sitting in their own homes, and he takes a great deal of trouble to persuade them that they want very much to see whatever picture is being shown. The manager on his job usually makes a practice of standing in his lobby after a show to get his patrons' comments as they go out, whether they make them to each other or straight to him. Often the patron and the manager praise or damn Hollywood together but there are some practices, much discussed practices, in the motion picture business for which the audience thinks that the manager ought to take full responsibility. Running advertisements on the screen, for one thing; bank night for another; free dishes; double features; and the revivals and reissues of old films. A good deal of the responsibility for these does actually belong to the exhibitor, though not so much perhaps as his patrons think.

Unlike radio, the movies are able to take their revenue directly from their audience. It is not essential, so far as the producer is concerned, to have a sponsor for a film in order to make it pay. Except for the previews of coming attractions, the advertisements thrown on the screen between pictures are of no value to the distributor. The theater man is the only one who benefits. In some cases there is even active objection to screen advertising. A great many local newspapers contend that they give the theaters far more space than they buy. Columns of publicity, printed without charge, are always added to the paid advertising for the current film at the local theater. If, by urging citizens into the theaters, the newspapers are going to cut their own advertising revenues from other sources they feel entitled to think themselves ill used.

The industry expresses its opinion in the matter not by indignation but by taking a high moral tone. To introduce advertisements into a show is to break faith with your patrons who have paid for entertainment. The magazine editor and his subscriber do not make a parallel case; the subscriber can skip the advertisements if he wants to; the moviegoer can hardly shut his eyes to the screen.

In their zeal for entertainment pure and uncontaminated the production companies have, since 1931, made a valiant effort to keep the names of advertised products out of their pictures. If an electric washer, a vacuum cleaner, or a tin of coffee is an essential property in a kitchen sequence the label is kept carefully concealed from sight. Only an expert can identify the brand. When the view from a restaurant terrace shows tall buildings trimmed with flashing electric signs, great care is exercised to see that none of those signs displays a registered trade-mark. Yet, so closely is advertising interwoven with American life and speech, it becomes impossible to banish it altogether from the screen. A whole series of gags may hang on your best friend's not telling you or on walking a mile for a Camel. A Rolls Royce or a Steinway grand may be a director's swiftest and most convenient symbol for sudden wealth.

Producers admit such infiltrations when art demands it but they were distressed when they found, by a survey made in 1937, that more than half the theaters in the country run advertisements on their screens. The Motion Picture Producers and Distributors of America have issued a statement recording their flat disapproval of the showing of advertising films. Some of the more important theater circuits forbid them on their screens. The theaters where they are shown are chiefly independents who find the proffered revenue too great to neglect. The price they receive for showing each advertisement runs from $2.50 a week to $25, depending on the size of the theater and its average attendance.

The vast majority of these films are advertisements for local firms but national advertisers are making such rapidly increasing use of the screen

that the Federal Trade Commission now scruti-
nizes their films as it examines newspaper, magazine, and radio advertising. Most of these national
advertisements are what are known as "minute
movies," very brief films, about as long as the previews of coming attractions, clearly and frankly
concerned with expounding the merits of a particular product. More subtle affairs are the "sponsored films"; the term is borrowed from radio
jargon. The sponsored film is one or two reels long
(ten minutes or twenty). Occasionally one runs an
hour. The idea is to make them just as amusing or
interesting as any standard short. The advertising
is introduced delicately. A bottle or a cake of soap
may take on a personality and become the hero of
an animated cartoon. A manufacturing process is
interestingly pictured in documentary fashion.
When an exhibitor can get, free, an expertly made
short which instructs and interests his patrons he is
very likely to take it. Sometimes, though the film
seems to him not quite good enough for his audience, he will submit to pressure from a neighborhood dealer who is selling one of the nationally
advertised products or from the local fire authorities who are interested in the lesson taught by an
insurance company's picture.

So far as anyone has managed to analyze the
attitude of the audience towards all this, they are
perfectly indifferent to injections of advertising in
their movie programs. What they do object to is

that, very frequently, the advertising films are dull.

The exhibitor may save a little money on sponsored films but he cannot fill his theater by running them. The desperate expedients of bank night, screeno, and free dishes are, as we saw in Chapter II, frowned upon by the industry as too basely commercial to be associated with art. The more correct method of offering them more for their money is the double bill.

The eighty-five million's attitude towards the double bill is a curious example of the imponderability of public opinion. Any moviegoer in any walk of life will damn double bills heartily if you question him alone; he will register his disapproval of them in a poll; but he will keep on going to the theater that offers him two features for the price of one. As soon as one theater in a community begins to run double bills the practice is practically forced upon the others. The instinct to get more for your money even when you do not particularly want it, is deeply implanted, apparently, in the American breast. Some theaters try to outbid their competitors by showing three features. One exhibitor, in Cody, Wyoming, is reported to have offered his patrons seven pictures for the price of one, an all-day performance starting at two-thirty and running until ten-forty in the evening. People came from all over the country, brought their supper, and stayed till ten-forty.

The second feature, or "program picture," in a

double bill is more cheaply produced than the first and usually not so good. It costs the exhibitor less to run it and it costs the audience less emotional strain to look at it. Theaters, however, which want to maintain a certain prestige in their communities, which like to be able to say that they never offer their patrons anything second rate, run two full-length important features on the same bill. This seems to a great many people a mental and emotional surfeit, certainly, repeated two or three times a week, a physical and nervous strain. It was as a public health measure that Chicago was urged to pass a city ordinance forbidding double bills. The Parent-Teacher Association which sponsored the idea is emphatic on the point that two hours and a half is quite long enough for any child to be indoors in a theater; the three- and four-hour programs of the double-feature shows are sapping, they say, their children's strength. The Parent-Teacher Association in Milwaukee took up the cry; so did the United Parents Association in New York City. The theaters politely forbore to suggest that it is the business of parents and teachers rather than of motion picture exhibitors to control the habits of the young but, as movements of the kind increase, the various branches of the industry are beginning to consider some form of their favorite "self-regulation."

In some communities theaters are coming to mutual agreement to abandon the practice of double billing. Some theaters, acting alone, are making proud boast of a single-feature policy. Still others are testing local sentiment by presenting single bills on certain specified days of the week. It is never safe to make prophecies about the movies but it seems not impossible that double bills are on the wane. The producers are no more enthusiastic about them than the exhibitors. They decrease the importance, and the rentals, of big films on which much money and effort have been spent. *Snow White and the Seven Dwarfs*, for instance, was leased only on agreement that it would be run as a single feature. In the summer of 1939 Warner Brothers created something of a sensation in the industry by announcing that it would not in future rent its pictures to the large and important Fox West Coast Theater chain. Those theaters make it a practice to run two big features on each program, which, Warner's alleges, is bad both for the prestige of the pictures and for their rentals. While there were some cries of joy over this cutting of the double knot, suspicion was also expressed that the true reason for the move was the desire of Warner's to detach itself from the chains, likely to be brought into disrepute or put out of business by the Government monopoly suit, and to win the good will of the independent exhibitors who may be the important customers of the future.

Another trade practice for whose success the exhibitors have much responsibility is the revival of successful films of the past, not the very long past, usually pictures of two or three years ago. In 1938 when the studios were cutting expenses at every corner they began to think wistfully of some of the successes of bygone years. There seemed to be no reason at all why a story which was a good story in 1934 or 1936 should not also be a good story in 1938 or even 1940. Plays are revived; books are reissued; why should films not have a longer life than the customary two and a half years? The theaters liked the idea. The films cost less and they drew. Exhibitors began enthusiastically to book revivals. They advertised "proven pictures," "tested films," "revivals of the fittest." People who had missed a much-talked-of movie on its original appearance were delighted at the chance to repair the omission; people who had seen and enjoyed a picture were often glad to see it again. Theater managers sent postcards to their patrons asking which old pictures they would like to see. Some circuits ran nothing but revivals.

Sometimes a picture was not "revived" but "reissued," remade with new actors and deletions or additions to suit contemporary taste. These films had harder sledding than the revivals for there were always critics with long memories to make invidious comparisons. In 1938 there were forty-five reissues, two hundred and forty-five revivals. The practice seems now to be fairly established and is another interesting instance of assistance offered to

the art by the industry. The primary motive for
revivals was economy but the survivors of a season
are likely to be better than the average picture,
and the sifting process will go on with the years.
If a film is really good it is well for the moviegoer
to see it a second time. One reason why it is difficult to acquire a knowledge of cinema technique
is because so seldom can one reread. Eventually
there will be pictures that every educated person
"must" have seen, just as he must now be familiar
with certain novels or symphonies or have watched
on the boards the plays of Shakespeare.

There is in the practice one possible minor danger. So rapidly do female fashions change in the
United States that ladies who in 1932 were glamorous leaders of fashion may look in 1940 more than
a little dowdy. Go back twenty years and a costume becomes quaint or picturesque; go back five
and it may be simply inappropriately funny. A
Louis XIV dress, however, or one of the 1860's is
equally good in any year after 1900. Will the
provident producer, thinking of the revival as well
as the first run of his films, be inclined to make
more of his big pictures historicals? And will that
be, or not, a good thing for the movies? So vast
and delicate is the art of the motion picture that
anything may alter its form, anything from a bustle
to an assistant attorney general.

VI

REFORMING THE MOVIES

ALMOST as soon as the first film had unrolled across the first projector zealots began to reform the movies. They have been reforming them ever since. From their birth the movies have had to struggle to establish their respectability. First they were told they were a menace to man's life; then to his morals; now to his social ideals. They are driven to one campaign after another to prove their innocence and repersuade the public that "motion pictures are your best entertainment." The history of the film is a series of fears, crises, and reforms.

Those champions of the motion picture who are stoutly maintaining today that it does not excite the young to crime have neglected the opportunity to draw an analogy from the first fear the movies inspired. The film fire scare was chiefly smoke. It began in Paris with a horrible conflagration at the Bazar de la Charité. This annual affair, dating

from the days of Marie Antoinette, brought together each spring all the scions of ancient houses
who looked back fondly to the days before democracy. On May 4, 1897, the newly perfected cinematograph made a much-appreciated addition to
the usual Bazar entertainment—until it burst into
flames. Those flames with hideous speed consumed
the flimsy temporary building jerried up for the
fair. One hundred and eighty spectators were
burned to death, and nearly every one of the one
hundred and eighty names was written in the Al-
manach de Gotha. Fashionable France went into
mourning and the story spread round the world.
The cinema took the blame. French motion picture production was set back at least a decade and
the fear of the highly inflammable nature of film
caused people everywhere to keep away from the
movies.

That fire was a factor in establishing the film as
an art for the people. It was so correct in Paris to
be related to some one who had died in the Charity
Bazar fire that there was a definite social *cachet* on
not going to the movies. Fear of fire kept nice
people away in other parts of the world, too; so
did dislike of bad air and of the lower classes beside whom one might be obliged to sit. Movies
were a cheap entertainment and therefore must be
bad. Nickelodeon became a derogatory term.

A dispassionate examination after the fact made
it clear at last that the real cause of the Bazar de la

Charité fire was the carelessness of the operator who had tried to refill the cinematograph's ether lamp by the light of a match; for the rest the temporary building rather than the celluloid was responsible. Actually motion picture film is no more inflammable than film for the ordinary camera which lies about casually in most households, but it took the industry many years to live down its dangerous reputation. Care and safety devices and fire laws are of course necessary but they have become now so standardized and automatic that no one expects to burn up at a movie any more than at a football game or in a train. Forty years after the Charity Bazar the industry was able to report that a daily interchange of twenty-seven thousand miles of film between five hundred exchanges and seventeen thousand theaters had gone on for years with almost no fire loss.

The moral reform of the movies is a longer story. One of Edison's early kinetograph pictures showed Annabelle-the-Dancer. The first story film, released in 1903, was *The Great Train Robbery*. The movies began almost at the beginning to traffic in sex and crime; and the reformers began almost at once their attempts to reduce the emphasis on those alluring and dangerous themes. In 1909 the first "better film society," the National Board of Review, was organized; in 1911 state censorship boards began to be set up. In 1922 the industry established its own moral regulating office. In 1934 the Catholic Church organized the Legion of Decency.

Each of these reforms was precipitated, quite appropriately, by a somewhat melodramatic crisis. It was the Charity Bazar fire which produced the safety reform. Ten years later, on Christmas Eve in the year 1904, Mayor McClellan ordered the police to close at midnight every nickelodeon in New York City. The reformers had found the movie an influence so demoralizing that it could no longer be borne.

The result of that midnight raid was the formation of the first organization for reforming the movies by kindness. The People's Institute, a civic bureau of social research and activities, set up the National Board of Censorship. This was a group of unpaid, socially minded individuals who undertook to preview films and disseminate information about them to everybody who would listen. The Board was established with the approval of the only organized group of motion picture producers then in existence. The producers agreed to make any changes or deletions the Board asked, even, if they insisted, to withdraw a film from circulation. For years the circular seal "Passed by the National Board of Censorship" was, not in New York City only but all over the country, the accepted stamp of purity. The Board was financed by a charge to producers of $3.50 (now $6.25) for each thousand feet of film reviewed, a sum which barely sufficed to pay overhead, office rent, and the salaries of secretaries. All the reviewers served without pay.

The Board did not like its name. It was adopted as a concession to the demands of the crisis, to persuade the public that, with films scrutinized by censors, the theaters might safely reopen. Actually the Board was emphatic in stating that it proposed to reform the movies not by censoring them but by educating their audience, by making people aware of what films might be if the best pictures were supported at the box-office by intelligent moviegoers. To the National Board would seem to belong the credit for the invention of "the intelligent moviegoer," that imaginary individual who has become almost as useful to social planners as the average man.

The Board's contention is that no individual or group can possibly decide for others what the moral effect of any work of art will be, what should be deleted and what condemned. Censorship, they hold, is definitely un-American. The real remedy is education. In 1916 they succeeded in changing their name to National Board of Review of Motion Pictures, which more accurately describes their function. The legend on their seal now reads "Classified and Passed," and classifying is what chiefly interests them. They indicate to potential audiences which pictures are good or particularly good and why, which are suitable for young people, which for little children. They publish weekly lists divided into "mature," "family," and "juvenile," with stars for pictures that are above the average, and "exceptional" against any film which has "outstanding cinematic qualities that make it a definite artistic contribution to the screen." They consider in their selections "entertainment, artistic, instructional, and ethical value." The industry has no objection to any of this. The more people talk about the movies the better, they believe; the terms in which they talk are a matter of secondary importance.

Fairly early in its career the National Board began to organize up and down the country Better Film Councils dedicated to the improvement of the movies by the improvement of local taste. Everyone must somewhere have encountered a Better Film Council. There are some six thousand of them. The correctly organized community today considers one as essential to its welfare as a Parent-Teacher Association, a Garden or Rotary Club. The difference is that the Better Film Council has as yet no stereotype. It is not possible to describe the genus, only some of the widely varied species.

There is, for instance, in a Southern industrial city a Council which was organized by the manager of the largest local theater. The energetic lady who did the organizing and keeps the Council running "for the cultural uplift of the community" is on the theater's pay roll. One cannot help suspecting that many of the "better films" that come to town will play the Palace Theater.

There is a Council in a New England city which publishes every week a succinct and disinterested little bulletin giving pertinent information about all the films playing in all the theaters. No attempt is made to rate or criticize, simply the facts are set down of cast and plot, director and décor, from which the intelligent moviegoer is expected to make up his own mind. Their handling of *Ecstasy* was characteristic. They told why New York banned the film and why Boston did not, commented amusedly on this reversal of the usual practice, and left the conscience problem to the individual spectator.

There is a theater manager in Ohio who never thinks of engaging a film for a special holiday or a children's matinée without consulting the local Better Film Council.

There is another in a New York suburb who ceased running double bills because the Better Film mothers did not like to have their children stay indoors too long at a stretch.

There is a theater manager in New Jersey who declined to pay any attention to his local Council's suggestions. He said they were a bunch of fool women with neither knowledge nor power. He was amazed to find them precisely informed about his company's organization, knowing how to carry their complaints to headquarters and to have him fired.

There is a mother in an Illinois town who will tell you that the whole family movie going is harmoniously and pleasantly directed by the lists of recommended films published weekly in the local newspapers.

There is another mother in the same community who, asked if her children read the "approved for juniors" lists, will answer that they most certainly do—and decline to go to any of those pictures. They say they are certain to be wholesome and dull.

There are Better Film Councils which are full of talk of the futility of their efforts and the lack of coöperation of exhibitors.

There are Better Film Councils which are convinced that they are the guardians of local culture and can show you statistically just how far the community intelligence quotient has risen since their organization.

The Better Film Councils do not all stem from the National Board of Review. Many of them are daughters of the Hays office, which has been so steadily increasing its activity of this kind that it is beginning to wonder whether the National Board has not outlived its usefulness and might advantageously let itself be absorbed. The interrelations and ramifications of the reformers by kindness are so complex that it is difficult for the layman to untangle them. Certainly no Better Film Council seeking guidance about organization, procedure, or "activities" need ever go astray for lack of advice. The National Board of Review, the DAR, the Association of University Women, the National Congress of Parents and Teachers, the General Federation of Women's Clubs, the National Council of Jewish Women, the International Federation of Catholic Alumnae are all concerned with bettering the cinema by improving its audience. They all have delegates who meet in Hollywood or in New York to preview films and issue lists which are circulated among their members, published in newspapers all over the country, and apparently widely read and heeded. In addition to this they publish magazines and bulletins and reports and reading lists and all the paraphernalia of any efficient American reform movement. Probably the most widely circulated of these lists is "Selected Motion Pictures," published by the Hays office East and West Coast Preview groups. "Selected Motion Pictures" goes every month to thirty-thousand civic leaders who disseminate its findings to local newspapers, radio stations, schools, clubs, churches. The Better Film groups are trying, too, as we shall see in the next chapter, to educate the younger generation to intelligent moviegoing by organizing Young Reviewers, 4-Star Clubs, Junior Councils, and motion picture appreciation classes in the schools.

Yet another group of reformers is trying to urge upon the film improvement not so much in technique as in ideas. Film Audiences for Democracy tries "to give Hollywood every encouragement to produce films that give a true and socially useful portrayal of the contemporary scene; to encourage production of films that will better the understanding between racial and religious groups; and to encourage the production of anti-war films." Conversely the Association is opposed to "any film portraying militarist, anti-labor or reactionary attitudes in a favorable light." Like the other reformers by kindness Film Audiences for Democracy preview pictures and distribute information about them to their members, but the questions the previewers are asked to answer have a different tang; not, "Would you recommend this film for church use? for schools?" "Is its artistic value excellent, fair, or poor?" but "Is the film militarist? anti-war?" "Are there any references to organized labor?" "Does the comic relief tend to caricature race? religion? nationality?" "Does the film depict unfavorable stereotypes?" The reviewers' reports carry such comment as: "Escapist and harmless diversion," or "an unimaginative and unhumorous handling of romantic comedy which glorifies a military and imperialist view point."

Not all the reformers by kindness by any means approve of one another. The devotees of the art-film, for instance, feel pretty strongly that most of the Better Film Councils are so concerned with decency that they forget about art, that they are elevating public morals at the expense of public taste. Better Film Councils, they point out, have three not altogether logical aesthetic convictions from which it is difficult to budge them. In the first place a better film to them is a clean film, a wholesome picture which can be marked unhesitatingly with the "family" classification. They suppose, too, that if the characters in a film expound, in word or action, high ideals, the picture is high art.

Then there is the belief that a film founded on a good novel or a good play is automatically a good film. From which it follows that a film founded on a great novel or a great play is probably a great film. The Better Film Councils conscientiously promote every movie version of Shakespeare. They are wide-eyed at the suggestion that the Astaire and Rogers' *Swingtime* was a finer picture than the Norma Shearer *Romeo and Juliet*, or that *The Amazing Dr. Clitterhouse* would repay study better than *David Copperfield*. So reverential is their attitude towards literature that they fail to make critical distinctions. To them—so the artfilm reformers charge—any book published more than fifty years ago is a classic. The screening of *The Prisoner of Zenda* is hailed as serious a promotion of the novel as the screening of *Tom Sawyer*, while every film that deals with history, even in the manner of *Marie Antoinette* or *Suez*, is to be studied as a contribution to culture. But the matter is by no means so simple as that. The industry does not agree with the artfilmers. It feels that at least one of the Better Film bodies, the National Board of Review, places all too much emphasis on art. Among the "exceptional photoplays" which the Board lists each month the proportion of foreign films to Hollywood films is so large that the *Motion Picture Herald* has viewed with alarm the Board's "frequent enthusiasm for alien and leftist expression on the screen." They think it curious, too, that the Board makes two lists of the Ten Best pictures of the year, one of the "best" and one of the "best on the basis of popular appeal." "That comes very near to saying," remarks the *Herald*, "that Hollywood knows best how to make pictures —for people."

The artfilmers are by their very nature unorganized though they sometimes gather into groups. I am using an arbitrary word to describe them for, unlike the other reformers, they have no accepted title. One of the cognomens applied to them is "montage boys," effectively descriptive of the general tone of their conversation. Their pet constructive remedies for the movies are two: the little theater for the specialized audience, and the independent producer who will be satisfied with a small profit. The theater and the novel, they argue, maintain their audiences on more than one level, why should not the movies do the same? Some of them see these experimental theaters offering their light to the producers-for-popular-consumption and gradually raising the whole level of the screen; others envisage an eternal gap between the movies for the masses and those for the initiated.

The same wave of reform which set all these improving-the-movies-by-kindness crusades in motion produced also state and municipal boards of censorship scattered irregularly about the country. Not so many were set up as the reformers wished; bills have been defeated in a good many legislatures, but there are now six state boards in active operation: Kansas, Maryland, New York, Ohio, Pennsylvania, and Virginia. There are also sixteen municipal boards—in Atlanta, Boston, Chicago, Charlotte (South Carolina), Dallas, Detroit, Kansas City, Los Angeles, Memphis, Milwaukee, New Haven, Oklahoma City, Philadelphia, Portland (Oregon), San Francisco, and Seattle.

This piecemeal method of control is of course quite unsatisfactory to the serious believers in censorship who can envisage a sane and safe screen only under the guidance of a federal censor. Bills to establish a federal censorship of motion pictures have been presented to Congress year after year and they have some zealous lobbyists, notably the Federal Motion Picture Council, the WCTU and various Protestant church organizations. Most of the reformers by kindness are dead against the idea, however, and so is the industry itself. Federal censorship is the only reform measure of which it seems to stand in real fear because federal censorship would undoubtedly imply a federal regulation of business practices as well. Towards the reformers-by-kindness the industry is complacent. The state and municipal censors it has, until recently, accepted fatalistically. They are an expense and a nuisance but it is not easy to disestablish a political censorship board once it has been set up; pleasant jobs, well paid and requiring no particular training, are useful things for a mayor or governor to have within his reach. The Hays office, with its hands upheld by the Legion of Decency, now does practically all the work which the state and city censorship boards were set up to accomplish, and for the average community the only necessity beyond that is the suppression of real indecencies by the police. But every censorship board thinks it incumbent upon it to take exception to a certain number of films every month in order to maintain its right to exist, and this of course makes trouble for the producers. Each of the major companies keeps a skillful and well-paid liaison officer whose duty it is to smooth the censors down so far as possible, to convince them that a shot which seems to them dubious in its effect will really not create the impression they fear, or that they can get the result they want by making a simple cut of a few feet instead of taking out a whole sequence.

Some of the handiwork of the censors is merely

silly, cutting shots of no intrinsic importance; some of it is annoying, blurring a sequence by omitting a necessary explanatory detail. That practice is particularly irritating to the states that border censorship areas. The same copy of a film must often do duty, for example, in Pennsylvania and New Jersey and the citizens of New Jersey are obliged to endure the ambiguities of Pennsylvania cutting without taking any pleasure, as the Pennsylvanians supposedly do, in being saved from sin.

To avoid so far as possible the expense and fatigue of this tinkering process the industry has informed itself carefully on the vagaries of each group of censors and manages in a great many cases to eliminate from the shooting script bits which are certain to be cut in one district or another. It is one of the duties of the Hays office to advise minutely on these points.

The complete lack of uniformity among the censorship boards would seem to be a proof of their arbitrary and illogical nature. Five of them will look with unoffended calm at a sequence which the sixth finds shocking. Some of the state boards have specialties. The Virginia censors are particularly concerned about sex. New York is more worried over political corruption. Maryland is afraid of anything which might stir up racial hatred or antagonistic relations between labor and capital. Kansas objects to drinking scenes and will not let anybody thumb his nose.

Not until 1939 did any of the "political" boards go so far as to condemn in its entirety a film bearing the seal of the industry's own Production Code. Early in that year the New York state board issued a ban against the showing of *Yes, My Darling Daughter*. *Yes, My Darling Daughter* treats the theory, not the practice, of free love and trial marriage. The movie version was decidedly milder than the play which had had a successful Broadway run without very much disturbing anyone. The critics of course cried out in unison against the censors' action; columnists bewailed the suppression of civil liberties; newspapers burst into editorials. Warner Brothers, producers of the film, appealed to the State Board of Regents and they promptly set aside the censors' ruling. A few excisions were made and the picture was allowed to run, much more dubious morally, the critics maintained, because suggestion was substituted for simple statement. The most important result of the incident was the introduction into the state legislature of a bill to repeal the censorship laws. Perhaps the "political" boards are not eternal after all.

Yes, My Darling Daughter was a rather mediocre film. Its disappearance would have been no great loss to the community. Occasionally of course the censoring, even by snippets, amounts to a real artistic crime, the mutilation of a masterpiece, but its most sinister effect is probably the suppression of ideas. Because Maryland has had a bonus march "incident" it may seem to her censors "inadvisable" to show in her theaters a scene of soldiers firing on a mob even though the setting be foreign and the action fictitious, as in *Three Men and a Prayer*. If Pennsylvania is fearful of Communism her censors will try to keep off the screen such forthright pictures as *Spain in Flames*, supposed to be pro-Communist because it is anti-Fascist. If Ohio has been suffering from strikes she will suppress the pro-labor *Million of Us*. There is no need to multiply examples; the fundamental principle of all censorship was laid down in 1930 by the British Board of Film Censors when they were confronted with Germaine Dulac's surrealist *La Coquille et le Clergyman*. It must be suppressed, said they, because it is "so cryptic as to be almost meaningless. If there is a meaning, it is doubtless objectionable."

No American censors are capable of a statement quite so sublime as that. They are immature as yet in the practice of their profession, not so sure of their objectives as the European censors, those straight onward striding men who not only control the film product of their own nationals but materially influence ours as well. It is they, for instance, who are largely responsible for the fact that 1938–1939, Motion Pictures' Greatest Year, became also motion pictures' most American year. Out of some 574 feature pictures 481 were tales of American life. Epics of our pioneer past, so popular as to constitute a cycle, flourished and the cinema began seriously to concern itself with America's present. Instead of Parisian night clubs, Swiss inns, and transatlantic liners, the screen is now filled with average American homes. Plots unfold in living rooms with ugly, inexpensive, comfortable furniture, in shabby dining rooms and servantless kitchens. This domestic trend appears to be related to the great wave of regional art and literature, the discovery of America by Americans, which is so important a cultural phenomenon of the nineteen-thirties. Its primary causes are, I think, two: the American public's growing desire for realism, for movies concerned with life as they know it—and the European censor.

The foreign market for American motion pictures is important. One hundred and fifty million people go to the movies weekly in the rest of the world, very many of them to see American films. The American industry has come to count on them for a large percentage of its profits, after the citizens of the United States have paid the production bill. The producer, consequently, will take a great deal of trouble to satisfy his European, Asiatic, and South American customers. Germany and Italy have both placed such heavy restrictions on American imports that the market there is practically dead but even so it seemed wiser to the trade to change the scene of *Idiot's Delight* to an anonymous country whose inhabitants speak not Italian but Esperanto. Since the British Board of Film Censors objects to humorous scenes in churches that 100 per cent American tale *Tom Sawyer* transferred its comedy to a meeting in the church basement. Masculine swimmers wear tops to their bathing suits in all continental releases. Buck Jones Westerns are toned down to prevent their overexciting the audiences in Singapore. RKO could not blow up the Thuggee temple in *Gunga Din* because the people of India object to seeing any place of worship destroyed. The whole picture was carefully watched by an English advisor lest any sequence run foul of Britain's colonial policy. *The Forty Days of Musa Dagh* was shelved at the command of Turkey. *Paths of Glory* was prohibited by France. Peru will have no scenes of rebellion against legally constituted authority. When *Beau Geste* was remade in 1939 the villains of the silent version (1926), Boldini and Lejeune, an Italian and a Belgian, were rechristened Rasinoff and Markoff. Film trade with Russia is small.

Films like those we have mentioned, dealing with political and social topics, might be expected to cause trouble but how is the producer to anticipate all the other difficulties raised by the foreign powers? How could he have imagined that Hungary would exclude *Green Pastures* as likely to "mislead the great masses with respect to the dogmatics of Christian religion"? Or that Mussolini would ban the Marx Brothers as "exemplars of the full flower

of anti-Fascist culture"? How could he foresee
when, searching for a disaster to compete with the
current earthquakes, hurricanes, and glaciers, he
scheduled *Titanic*, that the Cunard Line would
object, backed by the British Admiralty? How
could he anticipate the rage of the citizens of Oslo
at the Americanization of Sonja Henie? That rage
became fury when it was reported that Sonja had
taken out her first United States citizenship papers.
MGM soothed it by casting her in her next picture,
My Lucky Star, as a little Norwegian girl visiting America. To please the Japanese, Universal
changed a title announced as *Half Way to
Shanghai*. They made it *Sinners in Paradise*—as yet
unoccupied territory. One of the best of the apoc-
ryphal tales of Samuel Goldwyn credits him with
saying that he would like to film *Beverly of Grau-
stark* if he could be quite sure that it would not
offend any mythical kingdom. Is it a cause for surprise that the producer has retired for breath to
the American kitchen where he knows the arrangement of the furniture and can predict with
some assurance which topics are and which are
not safe for discussion?

The trend towards American domesticity is actu-
ated also by a desire to build up home trade as the
foreign market falls away. With the spread in
Europe and Asia of extreme nationalism the American film is being pushed out of its commanding
position in one country after another. The fact that

audiences like American pictures is of small account to a strong central government concerned either with cutting all films to the pattern of their particular national propaganda or else with the building up of a feeble native industry by protecting it from external, which means chiefly American, competition. The quota rules—what proportion of films shown in a country may come from abroad, the insistence that foreign companies make some of their films in the country where they are to be shown, the regulations about dubbing in sound track in the language of the land, the mounting taxes on the exhibition of imports are all aimed primarily at the universally too popular American film. More and more, therefore, the producer is concerning himself with building up bigger audiences in the United States and is letting Europe go. There are some half-tilled fields, too, in South America and other more distant quarters of the globe towards which he is beginning to turn interested eyes. Twentieth Century-Fox has opened offices in South Africa. A former consul is spending a million dollars on the construction of theaters in the Mexican provinces. *The March of Time* is getting out a special Dutch version of each reel for release in the Dutch East Indies. A fifteen-hundred seat Metro theater has been opened in Bombay and plans are under way for theaters in San Juan and Cairo. Popeye has appeared on a political poster in the Argentine. Paramount made *Tropic Holiday*

with popular Mexican musical stars and is following
it with other Latin musicals. Warner's is making
in Spanish and English historical shorts and the
United States Government is much interested, as
we shall see in Chapter IX, in increasing the number of our films shown in South America. The
industry thinks, too, that it has a working solution of the South American language problem.
The question has been which of the many variants
of Spanish to use. Each country dislikes films in
which the actors speak the dialect of another nation. If the scenes are set in the United States, it
has been discovered, nobody worries; the United
States is so extraordinary a country to the South
American mind that anything which happens there
is credible and the speaking of bad Spanish is not
annoying, as it would be in South America, but
merely part of the general fantasy.

Keeping track of what foreign audiences and
foreign censors want is one of the important duties
of the Hays office, that product of the next
great wave of American reform. That wave was
precipitated by the scandals, notably the Pickford
and the Arbuckle affairs, of the years just after
the Great War. By 1921 the press agents had got
the public pretty well excited about the Hollywood
stars. Movie actors were news and people felt a
right to demand that they live up to those standards of conduct set in a democracy for all public
characters. There was universal distress therefore

when Little Mary, the Nation's Sweetheart, went to Reno for a divorce from Owen Moore, married Douglas Fairbanks and then found the legality of her divorce being questioned. Worse still was the report of a party given in a hotel room in San Francisco by the fat comedian Arbuckle. A young actress died. She died apparently from an attack of a chronic ailment and three separate juries acquitted "Fatty" Arbuckle of anything more devilish than staging a drinking party; but the scandal sheets spread innuendoes so thick that the public suspected murder and filthy orgies, and no film of "Fatty" Arbuckle was ever again acceptable on the screen. Minor movie misdemeanors were played up by the press in the light of the two major shockers and the impression spread about the country that Hollywood was a great sink of vice. Something drastic and spectacular had to be done. The Motion Picture Producers and Distributors decided to follow the example of baseball and take to themselves a "czar"—the 1920 term for dictator—to purify the movies and pacify the public. They offered the job, with a $100,000 salary, to the Postmaster General of President Harding's cabinet, Will H. Hays. As campaign manager for Harding, Hays had been much interested in the vote-getting power of the newsreels and a good many movie magnates knew him well. His somewhat curious qualifications as a reformer did not become generally known until the 1928 Senate investigation of the Teapot

*Will H. Hays, President of the Motion Picture Producers and Distributors of America. His annual reports are **important social documents.***

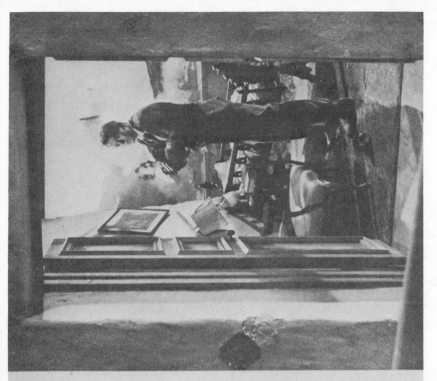

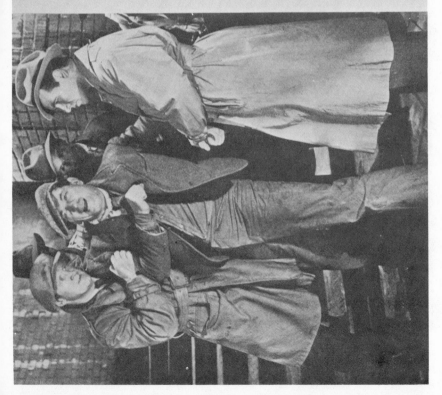

Foreign censorship: Peru prohibited the showing

Catholic censorship: Because "*Blockade*" excited

Dome scandal disclosed his complacent use for the Republican campaign chest of funds supplied by the notorious Harry F. Sinclair.

The activities of the Hays office have strengthened and developed with the years. There are offices in Hollywood, New York, Washington, London, and Paris. There is a Foreign Service Department, a Title Registration Bureau, a Theater Service Department, a Conservation Department working to reduce fire hazard. The most important parts of the work, however, are Community Service and the administration of the Production Code.

The advice to producers, at first a somewhat disjointed set of "don'ts" and "be carefuls," was elaborated in 1930 into the now famous Code. Many people of course had a hand in its making but the chief credit is claimed by Martin Quigley, publisher of motion picture trade papers, and Father D. A. Lord, S.J. The administration of the Code was at first in the hands of the executive secretary of the Motion Picture Producers and Distributors of America, Colonel Jason Joy. In 1934 he was succeeded by a member of his staff, Joseph Breen.

The producers were not at first too scrupulous in their respect for the Code's demands. When they lapsed from virtue they could too often justify the lapse by showing that it had brought in additional dollars at the box-office. It was not until the organization in 1934 of the Legion of Decency that box-office and Code became synonymous. "Resolutions for Uniform Interpretation of the Code as amended June 13, 1934" is the way it is stated officially. The Code is illuminating reading; it explains many curious elements in the American film.

CODE TO GOVERN THE MAKING OF TALKING, SYNCHRONIZED AND SILENT MOTION PICTURES

General Principles

1. No picture shall be produced which will lower the moral standards of those who see it. Hence the sympathy of the audience shall never be thrown to the side of crime, wrong-doing, evil or sin.

2. Correct standards of life, subject only to the requirements of drama and entertainment, shall be presented.

3. Law, natural or human, shall not be ridiculed, nor shall sympathy be created for its violation.

Particular Applications
I.   *Crimes against the Law*

These shall never be presented in such a way as to throw sympathy with the crime as against law and justice or to inspire others with a desire for imitation.

1. *Murder*
   a. The technique of murder must be presented in a way that will not inspire imitation.
   b. Brutal killings are not to be presented in detail.

   c. Revenge in modern times shall not be justified.

2. *Methods of Crime* should not be explicitly presented.

   a. Theft, robbery, safe-cracking, and dynamiting of trains, mines, buildings, etc., should not be detailed in method.

   b. Arson must be subject to the same safeguards.

   c. The use of firearms should be restricted to essentials.

   d. Methods of smuggling should not be presented.

3. *Illegal drug traffic* must never be presented.

4. *The use of liquor* in American life, when not required by the plot or for proper characterization, will not be shown.

II. *Sex*

The sanctity of the institution of marriage and the home shall be upheld. Pictures shall not infer that low forms of sex relationship are the accepted or common thing.

1. *Adultery*, sometimes necessary plot material, must not be explicitly treated, or justified, or presented attractively.

2. *Scenes of Passion*

   a. They should not be introduced when not essential to the plot.

   b. Excessive and lustful kissing, lustful embraces, suggestive postures and gestures, are not to be shown.

   c. In general passion should so be treated that these scenes do not stimulate the lower and baser element.

3. *Seduction or Rape*
   a. They should never be more than suggested, and only when essential for the plot, and even then never shown by explicit method.
   b. They are never the proper subject for comedy.
4. *Sex perversion* or any inference to it is forbidden.
5. *White slavery* shall not be treated.
6. *Miscegenation* (sex relationship between the white and black races) is forbidden.
7. *Sex hygiene* and venereal diseases are not subjects for motion pictures.
8. Scenes of *actual child birth*, in fact or in silhouette, are never to be presented.
9. *Children's sex organs* are never to be exposed.

III. *Vulgarity*

The treatment of low, disgusting, unpleasant, though not necessarily evil, subjects should be subject always to the dictate of good taste and a regard for the sensibilities of the audience.

IV. *Obscenity*

Obscenity in word, gesture, reference, song, joke, or by suggestion (even when likely to be understood by only part of the audience) is forbidden.

V. *Profanity*

Pointed profanity (this includes the words, God, Lord, Jesus, Christ—unless used reverently—Hell, S.O.B., damn, Gawd) or every other profane or vulgar expression however used, is forbidden.

VI. *Costume*

1. *Complete nudity* is never permitted. This includes nudity in fact or in silhouette, or any lecherous

or licentious notice thereof by other characters in the picture.

2. *Undressing scenes* should be avoided, and never used save where essential to the plot.

3. *Indecent or undue exposure* is forbidden.

4. *Dancing costumes* intended to permit undue exposure or indecent movements in the dance are forbidden.

VII. *Dances*

1. Dances suggesting or representing sexual actions or indecent passion are forbidden.

2. Dances which emphasize indecent movements are to be regarded as obscene.

VIII. *Religion*

1. No film or episode may throw *ridicule* on any religious faith.

2. *Ministers of religion* in their character as ministers of religion should not be used as comic characters or as villains.

3. *Ceremonies* of any definite religion should be carefully and respectfully handled.

IX. *Locations*

The treatment of bedrooms must be governed by good taste and delicacy.

X. *National Feelings*

1. *The use of the Flag* shall be consistently respectful.

2. *The history*, institutions, prominent people and citizenry of other nations shall be represented fairly.

XI. *Titles*

Salacious, indecent, or obscene titles shall not be used.

XII.   *Repellent Subjects*

The following subjects must be treated within the careful limits of good taste:

1. *Actual hangings* or electrocutions as legal punishments for crime.

2. *Third Degree* methods.

3. *Brutality* and possible gruesomeness.

4. *Branding* of people or animals.

5. *Apparent cruelty* to children or animals.

6. *The sale of women*, or a woman selling her virtue.

7. *Surgical operations.*

The Code means what it says. Because of Section III, "Vulgarity," for instance, Ethel Merman had, much against her will, to alter a line in "Heat Wave" when she sang it in *Alexander's Ragtime Band*. "Making her feet wave" was the Hays substitute for the original "Making her seat wave." Under Section II, "Sex," Gaby, *i.e.*, Hedy Lamarr, asked in *Algiers* with whom she is traveling, replies "My fiancé," surely a skillful translation of *mon ami*, though what code permits a young lady to go to Africa with her fiancé the Hays office did not explain. When the script of *Zaza* required a female character to shout "Pig! Pig! Pig!" at a gentleman admirer, the Hays office requested, "Delete two pigs." The list of words no screen actor may utter includes guts, nerts, louse, and sex appeal.

The Code seldom bends but there is a famous recorded instance where History and Patriotism

triumphed over Section V, "Profanity." After pro-
longed discussion it was decided that Warner
Brothers in making an historical short of Edward
Everett Hale's *The Man without a Country* might
permit Philip Nolan to say, "Damn the United
States!" Otherwise, it was pointed out, there would
be no story and the story teaches a fine lesson. In
most cases some ingenious way out can be found.
Twentieth Century-Fox, for instance, avoided the
dangerous implications of the title *Kidnapped*
(Section I, "Crimes against the Law") by carefully
referring to it always as Stevenson's *Kidnapped*.
The masterpiece in this kind probably was the fan
magazine handling of the Greta Garbo-Stokowski
affair. The Hays office has no direct authority over
the magazines but affects them by its control of
publicity stories from the studios and by its general
setting of the tone for the industry. "Garbo Finds
Love" was the fan magazines' theme and even between the chaste lines one could read nothing but
the purest romance. "Dwelling near him in a
flower-decked villa by the sea, with time to revel
in his company, is more bliss than she had believed
could ever be hers." "She continues to hide her
love behind words like friendship and companion-
ship." "Rumor is rife that they will be married.
Only time will tell."

Mr. Breen's task of administering the Code is
a work of heroic proportions. Every script of
every film is examined before the picture is shot,

and cuts and emendations are suggested in the large and in detail. Even before a script is ready producers begin asking advice on points which seem to them dubious. Again, because things get into a film in the making that were never contemplated in the script and because scenes give a different effect to the eye from that which they promised on paper, each finished film is carefully scrutinized before it goes out to the public. A member of the MPPDA (Motion Picture Producers and Distributors of America) who releases a film without the Breen seal of approval is liable to a fine of $25,000. Trailers, too, are inspected by the office; so are the stills and all the advertising, posters, press books, exploitation ideas, publicity stories. The number of each of these in a year runs into the tens of thousands.

The other important function of the Hays office, the Community Service, or public relations, division, is directed by the Secretary of the MPPDA, former Governor Carl E. Milliken of Maine. He and his associates are concerned with spreading good will from coast to coast, with answering everybody's questions, explaining away everybody's objections, coöperating in all possible directions. Anyone who wants to coöperate in any way with the motion picture industry will find a welcome at the Hays office. They are particularly eager to establish the movies in the upper cultural brackets and delight to work with those groups so frequently in the past ignored by the industry —schools, churches, libraries, women's clubs, social reformers of any stripe—whom the box-office and publicity men are likely to dismiss as minorities too small to be entitled to self-determination. The Hays office promotes the preparation of "study guides" on important films for classroom use. They help the companies to arrange "research exhibits" for libraries and museums. They supply speakers for the meetings of Better Film Committees. They receive with courtesy and efficiency writers on the movies, professional or otherwise.

The scope of the Hays office is great, so is its power but, like the moon, it does not entirely generate its own. Much of its force is derived from that most important and influential of all reform groups, the National Legion of Decency. The Legion has behind it not only the solemn authority of the Catholic Church but its genius for organization and its acute knowledge of just how far it is necessary to compromise with the forces it is combating. The Protestant Church, the Motion Picture Committee of the Federal Council of Churches, approached the industry as an investigator seeking to expose and reform. Its influence is not great. The Catholic Church proceeded by a wiser tactic.

The Legion was organized in 1934 when producers were finding themselves more and more steadily involved, without any particular intention or deliberate malice, in a contest of increasing smuttiness on the screen. When a touch of lasciviousness seemed to please the public it was logical enough to suppose that two touches would please them even more, and to proceed accordingly. Perhaps it was a cycle, like the gangster pictures or the glamour girl musicals. In any case the tendency seemed to be getting stronger and stronger, and by no means all the public liked it. Many of those responsible for the education of youth or the souls of a parish began to feel that going to the movies was becoming less a beneficial relaxation than a moral danger. The Church moved into action.

She took it for granted that the industry was no better pleased with the situation than she was and offered her coöperation towards improvement. She saw that the industry had already in the Hays office an instrument to her ends; she saw also that the instrument, though tempered, had no force behind it. That force the Church of Rome was admirably equipped to apply.

A crusade was preached and an Episcopal Committee of four appointed to direct it. They invited enrolment in the Legion of Decency whose members pledged themselves to attend only wholesome motion pictures. Protestants and Jews took the oath with the Catholics; so did women's clubs, civic organizations, the American Legion.

At weekly intervals the bishops issue lists of current films, indicating those which fall within and without the Church's requirements. Lists of this kind had been referred to by many good Catholics for years. In 1932 the International Federation of Catholic Alumnae began to preview films and issue comment in the manner of other Better Film Committees, and the movie going of many of their members had long been guided by their advice. The bishops asked them to continue and extend their work. The classification now in force is arranged with skillful flexibility. It offers appropriate guidance to every degree of intelligence and self-reliance.

Films are classified as A, B, and C. (There is an unfortunate confusion in this nomenclature with the commercial cost distinction between A and B films.) Class A pictures are those which are unobjectionable; anyone may see them, not necessarily with profit but at least without moral danger. Section I is listed as "unobjectionable for general patronage"; Section II, as "unobjectionable for adults." Class B pictures are "objectionable in part." They contain some sequence or situation or lines or plot element which is contrary to the teaching of the Church. Perhaps a story of courage and idealism, like *Ceiling Zero* or *Three Comrades*, presents suicide as an honorable solution of difficulties. Perhaps divorce is treated casually as it was in *Alexander's Ragtime Band*. Perhaps the dialogue is full of double-entendres. The Church does not wish to deny or conceal the existence of divorce or adultery or suicide or any other evil but it feels it important that they should be presented aesthetically from an orthodox point of view. To achieve this orthodoxy some artistic violence is occasionally necessary. When *Farewell to Arms* was reissued there was trouble over the unwed lovers with whom the audience must necessarily be in full sympathy. Finally it was arranged that the priest should murmur the marriage service beside the hero's hospital bed. The phrases in which the lovers thank him were rather obviously not from the pen of Ernest Hemingway but the film achieved a Class A rating.

The third list, the C, is very small. C pictures are flatly "condemned" and no member of the Legion may look at them.

With the weekly lists the Legion issues small printed slips "not for publication but for the confidential use of editors and subscribers." These give the reasons for B and C classifications. They run like this: "Class B, *Battle of Broadway*—Objections: Undignified treatment of marriage and immodest costuming." Or, "Class B, *Shape of Things to Come*—Objection: The Wellsian theory of a mechanical age with the exclusion of any thought of a Higher Being is expounded in this film." "Class C, *The Lie of Nina Petrovna*—Objections: Glamour created and sympathy induced for a lady of loose morals—story offers no compensating moral values—theme is immoral—suicide is plot solution."

Whether or not a member of the Legion of Decency should see a B picture is a matter between him and his own conscience. The bishops decline to rule upon that point. If a member feels himself sufficiently mature intellectually and morally to observe evil without contamination there is no reason why he should avert his eyes, but if he is young and pliable or if he prefers his entertainment unalloyed, without the burden and restraint of making decisions, he should confine his moviegoing to the A list. One of the convincing proofs the Legion offers of its effectiveness is the consternation that rises in New York when a film is shown before its classification has been published. All day long the office is besieged with telephone calls from loyal Legion members who want to go to the movies but will not under any circumstances attend a B or C picture.

It is immediately obvious that a Catholic Index of films has an influence upon the moving picture industry quite different from that of the Index Expurgatorius or the White List upon the publishing trade. The fact that his Catholic neighbor will not read *It Can't Happen Here* does not prevent the Protestant Mr. Jones from owning a copy but if all his Catholic neighbors announce their intention of staying away from C and B films the local theater will soon decline to run them and Mr. Jones will not be able to see them at any price. Since there are twenty million Catholics in the

United States the industry, with its guiding principle of the greatest happiness of the greatest number, finds it well worth while to regard their wishes, very clearly defined in terms of box-office. Though the Catholics are a minority group as compared to Protestants and Jews they are able by expert organization to make their peculiar prejudices prevail.

The Legion of Decency, like the censors and the majority of the Better Film Committees, is concerned not with the aesthetic but with the moral condition of the screen. For most of their purposes a clean film and a good film are synonymous. Many members of their preview committee are very competent judges of cinema technique but as Catholic Alumnae they are concerned chiefly with other issues. Mrs. James Looram, president of the International Federation of Catholic Alumnae, told me, for instance, with frank regret that they had been obliged to condemn to the C list *La Kermesse Héroique* (*Carnival in Flanders*), which she thought both highly entertaining and first-class cinema, because it showed "the end justifying the means" and because it dealt with "mass adultery."

The not infrequently repeated charge that the pressure of the Legion of Decency, and especially the presence in the Hays office of Joseph Breen, have acted to introduce positive Catholic propaganda into the movies, the Legion receives with tolerant amusement. They neither suggest to the industry nor urge them to do anything of the kind.

Sometimes, they suspect, a pro-Catholic bit is slipped in to divert their previewers' attention from something they might disapprove. Certainly when he makes a picture like the one about Father Flanagan's *Boys Town* the producer hopes for such support as that got by pastoral letter and radio address from the Bishop of Omaha and many other priests. It is quite possible, too, that a producer sees that he will please a large and vocal section of his audience by the introduction of a courageous priest or some particularly Catholic bit of morality. Nuns, when the context allows, are more picturesque on the screen than New England school teachers. If a sequence takes place in a church a scenic designer will naturally make the church as dramatically ecclesiastical as possible with altar and incense and candles. The Legion is very happy to see these things but it does not work for them. The principles for which it does work are very clearly set down in a little pamphlet *How to Judge the Morality of Motion Pictures*, which is authorized by the Episcopal Committee on Motion Pictures for the Legion of Decency.

The Legion of Decency [says the pamphlet] condemns obscenities of every kind in moving pictures. It condemns salaciousness—any appeal to the lower instincts of an audience, such as might be made by protracted and lustful intimacies between the sexes, by disrobing scenes or by other suggestive sequences. The Legion of Decency is governed by good sound common sense. It is not narrow-minded. While it agrees that the human body is beautiful it recognizes the serious moral danger to those seeing it exposed on the screen under attractive circumstances. It must condemn presentations introduced merely for suggestive display.

All these are highly important objectives. But the principal aim of the Legion is to discourage the production and patronizing of films which present false moral standards which, in turn, lower traditional morality.

By "traditional standards of morality" is meant such principles of conduct as the following: "Murder is wrong. Stealing is wrong. Perjury is wrong. Honor is due to father and mother." These standards, together with many relating to sex, follow from the code of right and wrong written into the conscience of men by God Himself. They have been generally known and accepted during all the centuries, not only by Christians, but by Jews, pagans, and by men of no religious affiliations. They are expressed in the Ten Commandments.

So careful is Hollywood to meet the Legion's requirements that the majority of condemned pictures are now of foreign origin. Curiously enough this does not include the Russian. On the first lists Russian films do not occur at all. Since they are entirely concerned, it was felt, with communistic, that is anti-God, propaganda, the best practice was to ignore them. The same attitude was adopted towards the American sponsored *Spain in Flames* and towards *Spanish Earth* which presented the case for the Loyalists. But in the summer of 1938 "Communism" appeared in a Hollywood film, *Blockade*. Walter Wanger who produced *Blockade* prefaced it with a statement that it was not intended as propaganda for either side in the Spanish War. What he was trying to do, apparently, although he did not say so, was to capitalize on the headlines as Paramount had done earlier in *Last Train from Madrid*. He was also, quite genuinely it would seem, making a plea for peace, one of the few "propagandas" to which the industry is wholeheartedly committed. Not even the most casual reader of headlines, however, could fail to identify the carefully unspecified enemy, the bombers of children and sinkers of food ships, with the forces of Franco, and the Church, which had steadily supported Franco, was alarmed. Here was an emotionally effective, if somewhat artificial, presentation of the case for those combatants whom they regarded as Communists, and therefore atheistic. The fact that the film showed peasant women lighting candles for the safety of their children and praying before the altar for the safe arrival of the food ship did not change their attitude. The Legion did not put *Blockade* on its C list. It added to its report for the week of June 30 a section "Separately Classified":

"*Birth of a Baby, The*—Observation: Unsuitable as entertainment for general theatrical exhibition.

"*Blockade*—Observation: Many people will regard this picture as containing foreign political propaganda in favor of one side in the present unfortunate struggle in Spain."

But the Church did not stop there. This case seemed so important as to demand more violent measures. According to Winchell Taylor, writing in the *Nation* of July 9, 1938, pressure was exerted upon the Catholic manager of Radio City Music Hall to prevent him from giving the film the important New York opening for which it was scheduled but the preview reports had been so enthusiastic that the manager felt under obligation to his box-office to resist the pressure and run *Blockade*. In Boston the City Council adopted a unanimous resolution expressing opposition to the showing of the film, but the mayor permitted it to appear with two deletions. The mayor of Somerville, Massachusetts, banned it. The Kansas City censors tried, unsuccessfully, to eliminate the hero's concluding speech. The commissioner of licenses in Providence, Rhode Island, refused a license for a second run although the film had already shown there in June. Most serious of all financially, the Fox West Coast Theater chain, under Catholic pressure, refused to run *Blockade* as a regular first feature. So large is that chain that to be forced by it to take the smaller rental accorded to a second feature may well kill an A picture. *Blockade* continued to be seen about the country, but Mr. Wanger canceled the anti-Fascist *Personal History* of Vincent Sheean which he had been about to make when the opposition began.

This belligerency, open and secret, marked a change in the Legion's policy. "Communism" is no longer to be ignored but openly combated. This was made quite clear by a statement issued by the bishops in August, 1938. They expressed to the industry their appreciation of the general improvement of the films in moral character and tone and then went on to say:

The Legion views with grave apprehension those efforts now being made to utilize the cinema for the spread of ideas antagonistic, not only to traditional Christian morality but to all religion. It must oppose the efforts of those who would make motion pictures an agency for the dissemination of the false, atheistic and immoral doctrines repeatedly condemned by all accepted moral teachers,

Films which portray, approvingly, concepts rooted in philosophies attacking the Christian moral order and the supernatural destiny of man serve not to ennoble but, rather, to debase humanity, and as such, these films are an affront to right thinking men and women,

The Legion of Decency, with every resource at its command, shall challenge any program using the popular theater screen to exploit such insidious doctrines. Secular affairs are not in themselves the concern of the Legion of Decency. When, however, contrary to all that is truly American, unchanging principles of morality are assailed and atheism and irreligion are fostered, the Legion must, in pursuit of its single and unvarying objective of a morally wholesome screen, interpose the full weight of Catholic opinion and authority.

The warning to producers is clear. The Catholic Church is the chief guardian of the American screen. The Church will tolerate on that screen other religions but, not, despite the freedom of thought permitted by the American Constitution, any point of view which seems to run counter to "traditional morality" as defined by the Catholic Church.

Of the forces attempting to reform the motion picture the Legion of Decency is most to be reckoned with in the future. Its national power has only begun to be felt, and there is an international power to come. The Legion is now a member of L'Office Catholique International du Cinématographe, a federation of Catholic motion picture organizations which embraces some twelve countries. Their purpose is to strengthen the Catholic world front in the motion picture field. It is the most deliberate attempt which has yet been made to control the American screen in the interest of a group.

The influence exerted upon the screen by Wall Street is more difficult to trace. Rumor has it that orders come down from time to time directing that this story be abandoned or that theme emphasized. Perhaps the Government monopoly investigation will show whether the control is really specific or only general. Undoubtedly the fact that the movies are a billion-dollar industry serves to make the average film an advocate of the "American way," to make it a defender, even when it is only froth or nonsense, of the *status quo*.

We may not have Federal censorship in America but the American movie certainly does not want for attention, regulation, and advice.

VII

TAKING THE MOVIES SERIOUSLY

M OTION Pictures' Greatest Year, the two World's Fairs, and the current pastime of resurrecting our national past have produced recently several film histories of the films. They are fascinating documents, whether you began your movie going in the '90's or in 1936, but the chronological method which all of them use does not seem the ideal approach. A history of the movies should not be a documentary film but a melodrama. The proper plot for any Cavalcade of the Motion Picture is that favorite movie plot, the Cinderella story. From Nickelodeon to Billion-Dollar Industry; From Converted Shooting Gallery to Radio City Music Hall. From the little theater on the side street which no nice woman could be seen entering to the Broadway première attended by statesmen, artists, and the most luminous names in the Social Register.

There are not many imaginations in the United States capable of assembling that scenario but it ought to be done. It might be accomplished by teamwork, some such combination, say, as Pare Lorentz, Cecil DeMille, and Walt Disney. In any case, whoever makes it, there will be one scene that shows the movies crashing the gates of learning, not just one pair of gates but a whole avenue of them stretching across the country from west to east.

The gates went down almost as suddenly as the walls of Jericho. Three years ago a survey made under the direction of the United States Commissioner of Education could discover only fourteen colleges which admitted the existence of the art of the motion picture. In 1939 the annual report of the President of the Motion Picture Producers and Distributors of America made quiet note of the fact that fifty-three institutions of higher learning are offering for credit complete courses in some aspect of the movies and two hundred others admit movies by some door into their curricula.

In a country whose universities teach baseball coaching, embalming, and hotel management it is not of course to have arrived academically to get into a college catalogue. It is where you are in the catalogue that counts. In their capacity as an industry paying $100,000,000 a year in taxes the movies appear in the courses of a good many business schools. You may learn specifically how to distribute films or how to manage a theater, or you may gather from the lips of magnates an outline of the problems of the industry. Some universities offer instruction in motion picture photography and lighting. Others give courses in scenario writing. These are presented, like most college work in play production and the writing of short stories, as a mixture of vocational training and the culture to be derived from a practical acquaintance with the technique of an art. Sometimes the motion picture appears in college bulletins under "Education," more frequently under "English," that stalwart subject having already assimilated another academic parvenu, the drama. The most exalted academic position so far attained by the movies is in the Columbia University Catalogue announcing courses for 1939–40. Under "English and Comparative Literature," between "Beowulf" and "English Literature from the Beginning to the Death of Shakespeare" stands this notice:

Eng. 49-50—History and art of the motion picture. Research and conferences. 2 points each session and 2 maturity credits each session. Dr. Emrich. Tu. and Th. at 10: Registration is limited to 15 students. Permission of the instructor must be secured before registering. Members of the course must hold themselves in readiness once a week to attend exhibits and projections at various points in the city. Prerequisites: At least 18 points of credit in Eng. and Comparative Lit.

Columbia has for several years had extension courses in the motion picture but this is probably the first time any college has treated it as a research subject.

The most usual title for courses in the film is "Motion Picture Appreciation." That unhappy term should not be held against the movies. For years reputable institutions of learning have been teaching Art Appreciation and the Appreciation of Music. The movies are simply following an academic fashion. In most instances these appreciation courses have appeared in response to a real popular demand. Every year more and more people are taking the movies seriously. The first time that Columbia offered an extension course in the film, under the auspices of the Museum of Modern Art, there were five times as many applicants as it was possible to teach. Some of the appreciation courses are very general in nature, a series of lectures given by experts in different sections of the industry but without any particular interrelationship. Sometimes critical comment and explanation accompany the showing of significant films. Sometimes, as in the usual college course in literature, a single instructor lectures and directs the study. Some courses are concerned primarily with the film as art: "History of Films to 1915," "Basis of Film Technique." Others deal with its social relationships: "The Public Library and Motion Pictures," "The Film as Journalism and Entertainment," "The Motion Picture and the Masses."

A great many of the students in the appreciation courses are school teachers preparing to impart motion picture appreciation to their pupils in high or grammar school. The Hays office calls it a conservative guess that six thousand of the country's schools now include the movies among their academic subjects. They have made their way into the schools through the progressiveness or, if you prefer, the pusillanimity of the American teacher; either because she is quick to make use of any new device that presents itself or because, since children are interested in movies anyway, it seems simpler to teach movies than Latin or the English classics. Whatever its cause the industry is pleased by the school connection and is working to strengthen it. With "study guides" and "research exhibits" and information about current films they are delighted to coöperate with the teacher who is trying to show her motion picture appreciation class why the picture at the local theater this week is an important movie or with the history teacher who wants to use it to stir youthful curiosity about Andrew Jackson or the French Revolution.

The industry is interested also in supplying films for the 16 mm. projectors which are fast becoming part of the essential equipment of every up-to-date school. The Motion Picture Producers and Distributors of America have helped the National Education Association to finance various surveys on the value of "pedagogic films." Catalogues recently issued list several hundred produced by the motion picture companies with the suggestion and advice of educators. In the summer of 1939 the movies and the teachers announced a joint project for the use in schools of old theatrical films.

The life of the average movie, as we saw in Chapter V, is about two and a half years but that is only an arbitrary commercial life span. Age does not actually lessen the beauty of a travelogue or the value of pictures of lumbering in the North Woods or the exemplary habits of the beaver. The producers have agreed to put old films of this kind at the disposal of the schools and an energetic committee has already examined some twelve hundred and recommended about half as suitable in their present form for classroom use. Prints of these have been made on 16 mm. film and are now available at very low rates to teachers of geography, history, the sciences.

That is only half the story. "Human relations and social adjustment" are to be taught by excerpts made from out-of-date feature films. The idea is to select and piece together sequences which present problems of conduct: should she have married him? was it right to disobey her mother? was that lie justified? The picture is shown to the class and then they discuss the situation under their teacher's guidance. "This project," said Mr. Hays addressing the Seventy-seventh Annual Convention of the National Education Association, "is an endeavor to take into the school a preview and practice of life itself, a rehearsal for conduct both now and after graduation."

This is to take the movies very seriously indeed and the industry is preening itself upon its public recognition as a moral teacher and instrument for good. The project is an elaborate one. It began about ten years ago when, to quote Mr. Hays, a "volunteer committee of specialists" with the co-operation of the Motion Picture Producers and Distributors of America arranged a set of twenty short films made up of

excerpts selected from existing photoplays, each presenting a real life situation, available in the classroom for study and discussion under the guidance of a trained leader, in order that pupils while still in school may be better equipped to meet the emergencies which they will later confront in actual life. During the years from 1934 to 1936, under the direction of this committee, nearly 50,000 discussion demonstrations were conducted in 17,000 separate school groups located in 81 cities. More than 500,000 school pupils participated in one or more of these discussions. The success of this work led directly to its expansion under the Commission on Human Relations of the Progressive Education Association.

About seventy-five of these "human relations short subjects" are now available to schools.

The general studies made by the Commission prior to this experiment indicate that an American youth passing from childhood through adolescence to adult development has to adapt himself to some 175 difficult human relations situations. These transitions are imposed on him or required of him by the culture into which he is born. It is an educational responsibility to aid him in making these adaptations. It is an educational opportunity to give him an understanding of why the adaptations are required. From the social welfare standpoint, it is of the highest importance that these responsibilities be fulfilled during the course of formal education in the schools. Out of these 175 critical situations, it is believed that approximately 100 can best be approached and understood through the film discussion method which was developed by the Commission.

The movies can now say that they are accepted as moral mentors, as visual educators, and as art. They have college catalogues to prove it. They may also say that they are history. There are museum catalogues to prove that. Go, for instance, into the Cabildo, the magnificent museum which guards the rich wealth of New Orleans' history. Prominently displayed among its treasures is the shooting script of *The Buccaneer*, locale New Orleans, presented by no less a person than the director of the film, Cecil B. DeMille.

Or go into the Motion Picture Museum on the Steel Pier at Atlantic City. It looks like any small-town historical museum, a big room lined with glass cases filled with dresses, swords, furniture, watches, jewels. But, instead of being Colonial and Civil War with perhaps a touch here and there of late Victorian, the costumes and the properties are renaissance, oriental, modern, of any race and any time. Each article is labeled reverently in the tone the folk museum uses for the pen which was actually used by George Washington or the button some daring lady clipped from the sleeve of Lafayette: This dress was worn in [such and such a picture] by Norma Shearer. That sword was drawn by Clark Gable. That chair appeared in the great banquet scene in *Robin Hood*. The spectators respectfully and interestedly gaze and point and discuss.

Sometimes a particularly important motion picture assembles a little museum of its own. The most impressive collection so far acquired belongs to *Marie Antoinette*, a film which laid great stress on its importance as an historical document. The picture opened in New York. For weeks beforehand the Astor Theater, where it was to be shown, was converted into a museum. Purple velvet draped the walls and set off the collection: furniture, costumes, jewelry that had been used in the film. Some of the articles were skillful reproductions, many of them actual eighteenth-century pieces imported from France. They were insured for $100,000. The *Marie Antoinette* Museum had a private opening, by invitation only, on Bastille Day. After that its doors were flung wide, quite free, to the public. They came, more than 200,000 of them in three weeks.

The most famous of all motion picture museum pieces is probably that in the Los Angeles Museum of History, Science, and Art. It was presented by a very popular star. The director invited the gift because he thought that its presence in the museum would attract visitors, who might then be interested in other exhibits. Displayed by itself, in a special case set in an important position, is a small Tahitian garment—the sarong worn in *Her Jungle Love* by Dorothy Lamour.

Other museums, with a slightly different point of view, are also concerned with conserving the art of the motion picture. In New York the Museum of Modern Art Film Library has begun the much-needed work of saving the early masterpieces of the screen which were fast decaying unnoticed or being actually destroyed to make room for the output of today. Until the revival idea started—it has been discussed in Chapter V—a three-year-old movie was for all practical purposes dead. You could read of landmarks in screen history but, unless your memory was long and your experience wide, you had small idea what they looked like. In 1930, with the aid of a grant from the Rockefeller Foundation, the Museum began to acquire and preserve old films and current ones which they thought "noteworthy." When the producers found that they were being treated seriously as creators of "classics" their pride was stirred; they gave their warm coöperation. The Museum now has in its collection more than seven hundred films, American and foreign, running from the earliest days to the present.

Towards this collection the Film Library has the modern museum attitude. These films were not gathered to be hoarded in their cans. The chief purpose was to make the eighty-five million Americans familiar with the art they are helping to create, to make the unconverted millions realize how important a section of American life they are neglecting. The Museum patiently and skillfully made fresh prints of selected early films, arranged them in related groups, and began to circulate them about the country. They are accompanied by elaborate printed programs, very interesting and illuminating to read, which treat even Harold Lloyd and Mickey Mouse with high seriousness as significant phenomena in the history of a great art. The interest the antique films created was an indication of the growing seriousness with which the public is taking the movies. Schools, colleges, one community after another wanted to see the film series, and having looked at one asked for more. Last year the Museum's films were shown in one hundred and seventy-five institutions.

When an audience looks at a primitive film they usually find it hilariously amusing and nothing more. The rapid and jerky action, the high wind, the theatrical gestures which have not yet learned to subdue themselves to their medium, the crude plots, the dated costumes, the glamour of another day, are all very funny—at first. After a time the spectator finds himself seeing a great deal more than that: effects of beauty or humor or suspense obtained by doing with motion and light and shadow things that could not be done in any other medium; the camera beginning to learn its power; a director imagining and inventing with no precedent to follow. At the beginning of a film series the audiences come out laughing; at the end they are talking excitedly in the kind of terms one uses to discuss early music or primitive painting.

These film series are not confined to the American motion picture; they assemble early masterpieces from France, from Germany, Italy, Russia, Sweden, Denmark, tracing influences back and forth. Now the Museum of Modern Art is affiliated with the International Federation of Film Archives composed of the Cinémathèque française, Paris; the Reichsfilmarchiv, Berlin; and the National Film Library, London. Other nations are preparing to join. At a conference held in New York in the summer of 1939 representatives were present from Argentina, Brazil, Chile, Japan, Italy, Denmark, Sweden, and Switzerland. The central office of the Film Archives is in Paris in the Palais Royal, quarters made available by the French Government. The United States Government is assisting the project by admitting old films to this country duty free. "This International Federation of Film Archives," said John Abbott, director of the Museum of Modern Art Film Library, "marks a great step forward in the task of preserving the important films of the world. It is a significant recognition of the international importance of the film as a record of contemporary times." Phrases like that ring pleasantly to the former nickelodeon.

The movies, like the other great arts, have now their professors, their curators, their archivists; they have also their private collectors. The fashion of collecting motion-picture stills began in Los Angeles but it is spreading over the country. Historians will one day arise to call these "still collectors" blessed. For an age that digs up all the past and records in print or pictures its own every motion, we are singularly prodigal of records. We make them but we throw them away. For every movie they produce which is of the least importance the companies make hundreds of stills, not cuts from the film but carefully posed pictures of groups and scenes. Once a picture is taken, striking off duplicate prints is a comparatively inexpensive matter; they are made with a prodigal hand. They are designed for publicity purposes, to illustrate magazine and newspaper articles, to dress up advertisements, to adorn the fronts of theaters. When they have done their work it is a matter of indifference to the companies what becomes of them.

They are seldom needed again. Some producers make a practice of destroying negatives a year or two after a film goes out of circulation. Scenes from bygone pictures, portraits of once-beloved stars sift into the second-hand bookshops and the junk piles of dealers in antiques. They can be bought usually for a few cents apiece.

There is a story that the Hollywood vogue was started by one Henry Pierson who, purchasing his first batch of stills by mere chance, became interested in the possibilities of the game and began to buy up pictures wherever he could lay hands on them. When he had too many duplicates he sold or gave them to his friends, starting them on the collector's path. Presently his collection became so large that he was obliged to restrict his interest. He decided to specialize in pictures that had won Motion Picture Academy awards. He now has about twelve hundred stills, probably the largest private collection in the country. He is outranked, he thinks, only by institutions, the Museum of Modern Art, the New York Public Library, and Harvard University.

Once you could buy any old stills you found in a book shop ten for a penny. Now the dealers are learning to make distinctions. There are standard prints and there are collector's items. For a W. S. Hart, an early Mary Pickford, or a scene from *The Great Train Robbery* it may be necessary to pay as much as five dollars. A set of forty stills from Griffith's *Birth of a Nation* recently sold for a hundred dollars. Any still older than 1920 is considered rare.

Stills, scenarios, shooting scripts, all these are preserved by the museums and libraries which of course have for years assembled books about the film. Now the movies have advanced to the dignity of a voluminous scholarly bibliography. Compiled by the Federal Writers Project, *The Film in America—a Bibliography* is being published in three volumes by the H. W. Wilson Company and the Museum of Modern Art Film Library. Volume I, *The Film as Art*, appeared in the fall of 1939. It includes nine thousand book and magazine references, with brief digests of each, and reviews of three or four thousand pictures from *The Fred Ott Sneeze* of 1887 to *Snow White and the Seven Dwarfs*. The other two volumes, *The Film as Industry* and *The Film in Society*, will not be ready for another year or two.

The learned institutions, as we see, are distinguishing the movies by giving them their serious attention; they are beginning to distinguish them also by decorating them with badges of honor. The country was a trifle surprised, though more than a little delighted, when in the same June, 1938, Yale, Harvard, and the University of Southern California granted to Walt Disney honorary masterships of science and art. In the same month the Vice President and General Counsel for Metro-

Goldwyn-Mayer, J. Robert Rubin, received from Oglethorpe University an honorary doctorate of laws. June, 1939, saw Martin Quigley, publisher of the *Motion Picture Herald* and other trade journals, receiving from Loyola University in Los Angeles an honorary Litt.D. with a citation which left no doubt in any mind that the motion picture is now taken seriously both morally and academically.

He it was [the phrases ran] who conceived and later saw to the preparation of the motion picture Production Code of Ethics which is now the Magna Carta that serves as a practical working guide of moral principles for those engaged in the production of motion pictures in the United States. He it is who "fought the good fight" for decency in motion pictures, for proper moral standards by which these pictures can be made to entertain without, at the same time, perverting those principles of Christian morality upon which great nations must build if they are to survive.

Set that beside the fact that the Pope has made the administrator of the Production Code, Joseph I. Breen, a Knight Commander of the Order of St. Gregory, and it becomes apparent that not education only but the Catholic Church is taking the movies seriously.

And personal honors to movie magnates and artists are not the end. America has begun to mark with tablets the sites of historic moments in the life of the motion picture. The first enduring brass is attached to the 34th Street side of R. H. Macy's store. With speeches of dedication it was unveiled by the widow of Thomas Edison. It reads:

"Here the Motion Picture began. At this site, on the night of April 23, 1896, at Koster and Bial's Music Hall, Thomas A. Edison's motion pictures were projected."

That unveiling ceremony might make a good climax for the Cinderella story of the cinema.

VIII

THE VAMPIRE ART

PLEASED as the movies are with their serious reception in the halls of learning they are even more pleased when they find themselves admitted to the sisterhood of the arts. It is the state of mind of the little girl who wants to be grown up. The movies are barely fifty, absurdly young for any art, and their sisters are only too apt to belittle their commercial success by questioning their claim to being an art at all.

When Adolf Zukor had the notion of raising the motion picture's standing by presenting films of "Famous Players in Famous Plays," importing the four-reel *Queen Elizabeth* made by Sarah Bernhardt, starring James K. Hackett, in *The Prisoner of Zenda,* he created a fear which is still rampant, the fear that the movies are a vampire art battening on the drama and the novel, on music and the dance, draining away their artists and their audiences, leaving them mere crumbling shells. So cheap, say the fearful, and so readily accessible are the young art's palaces, that anyone may contract the vicious habit of movie attendance and awake one day to find his taste for true theater gone. More ominous still is the foreboding that young people who spend their time at the pictures will gradually cease to read. Soon, it is predicted, they will think that reading requires too great an effort; they will prefer to absorb their necessary ration of romance, adventure, and instruction through the painless medium of the screen. The evenings which used to be devoted to curling up with a good book will now be spent in the foul air of the local Alhambra or Garden.

There is alarm, too, lest the vampire suck away the strength not only of audiences but of artists. Are not the fantastic salaries of Hollywood drawing the best of our actors from Broadway to the Coast, where their talents will inevitably be prostituted? About novelists and story writers there is some worry but rather less; any writer who really wants to prostitute his talent has plenty of efficient publishing media in which to do it.

The movies are doing their valiant best to allay the terrors of the guardians of culture. They ask them to listen for a moment to the voice of Broadway crying out to Hollywood to finance its plays or to watch the spectacle of schoolteachers, hundreds of schoolteachers, urging their charges to the movies as the surest way of inducing them to read the literary classics. Music and the dance, they claim, are looking gratefully towards the screen while the cinema even holds out a charitable hand to sculpture and painting. Far from preying upon the other arts the movies believe that they are nourishing them. Are they right, and if they are, how wholesome is that nourishment they are so proudly furnishing?

When the dramatists and the motion picture producers quarreled in 1936 and severed relations for a year or so the point of contention was the division of profits; there was no doubt in anyone's mind that there were plenty of profits to divide. The movies like to film plays that can be ticketed "Broadway success." Those words are still magic in the provinces and there are other assets besides. A good deal of advance advertising is done on the title and the story has been proved against an audience. It is actually cheaper for Hollywood to test the popular appeal of a drama by producing it in the theater than by making a film of it and finding it falls flat. On the dramatist's side there is the obvious advantage of enormously larger profits than he could make in the theater alone. When a playwright can get $275,000 for screen rights, as Robert Sherwood did, for instance, for *Abe Lincoln in Illinois*, he can write to suit himself, if he wants to, for the rest of his life. Sometimes the screen's assistance to the theater comes a little more indirectly. When his *Paradise Lost* was failing on Broadway, Clifford Odets went out to the Coast and wrote for the movies, sending his salary back to New York so that the Group Theater could keep the play going. Franchot Tone, too, has used his movie salary for the support of that important experimental company with which he likes to act.

There is of course in all this mutual give and take a danger to the theater; the dramatist is too often tempted to write with one eye upon the screen, omitting situations that might not be acceptable in Hollywood or introducing others merely because they would make good movie material. It cannot be said too often that the theater and the motion picture are separate and distinct arts and no one needs more constantly to remember this than the men who serve them both, yet, even in the face of this grave peril, the movies can make a strong case for themselves as a nourisher rather than a destroyer of the stage.

The vampire feeds the actor, too. The high salaries Hollywood is able to offer Broadway stars are not necessarily occasions for grief. The techniques of stage and screen acting may not be the same but they need not destroy each other. Plenty of distinguished stage players shuttle between New York and California and thoroughly enjoy acting for the movies. Hollywood serves also as a kind of old-age pension for the deserving. Bit parts in

films, good bits, are waiting for the expert of almost any vintage. When a minor scene in a movie
kindles suddenly into reality, a reference to the
cast list will almost invariably show some name
that still echoes on Broadway. A California sunset
of life looks to most aging actors very much pleasanter than barnstorming the country in one-night
stands. And the stream flows both ways. The more
intelligent and earnest of the players who have
grown up with the films are beginning to sense the
advantages of stage experience. Every year Hollywood pours out upon the country potential talent
seeking experience in stock or summer theater.

So far as audiences are concerned the movie
may be charged with the strangling of vaudeville
but it does not seem to have garrotted the theater.
There are fewer stock companies, perhaps; slightly
fewer road companies than there used to be; but
amateur groups are everywhere; we have had a
flourishing Federal Theater; and there are the ubiq-
uitous summer playhouses. The movies can hardly
be accused today of having killed the stage though
it may not be possible to prove that they make
people go to the theater as it is quite definitely
proved that movies make people read books.

In the early days of antagonism to the movies as
the great enemy of reading the case for the book
was always presented on moral grounds. Books are
ennobling; movies debased. Books instruct; movies

present children with idle and vicious ideas. Nickel-
odeons were places from which the young needed
to be saved, like saloons and poolrooms.

Then the movies began to mount the ladder of
prestige. As they screened important novels and
successful plays they began to take on the respectability of the originals. Teachers and parents were
reluctantly impressed, but immediately they developed a new fear: might not the child who had
seen a classic on the screen think that he knew all
about it? Might he not feel it quite unnecessary
to read the book?

That fear, too, is melting, melting because it is
becoming perfectly obvious that the more children
go to the movies the more they want to read books.
The quickest way of interesting your pupil in a
biography or a history or a novel seems to be to
connect it with some picture he has recently seen
or is about to see.

For a long while the teachers were wary of
accepting their own evidence—it looked too easily
pleasant to be true, but they are being borne down
by a mass of steadily accumulating facts. A high-
school teacher in Memphis, for instance, has it on
grateful record that Ronald Colman in *If I Were
King* set her seniors to reading and learning by
heart the ballads of François Villon. New Orleans
school children were driven to enthusiastic research on local history by the opening of *The
Buccaneer*. A Superior, Wisconsin, high school had

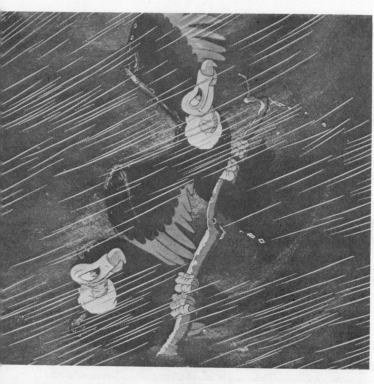

Movies and pictures. Movies are now officially art. A gouache on celluloid from Walt Disney's "Snow White" hangs in the Metropolitan Museum.

Movies and books. Movies make people read books. One of the devices by which the Cleveland Public Library enlists their coöperation.

Movies and music. The scores American composers are writing for films are of more musical importance than the appearance on the screen of

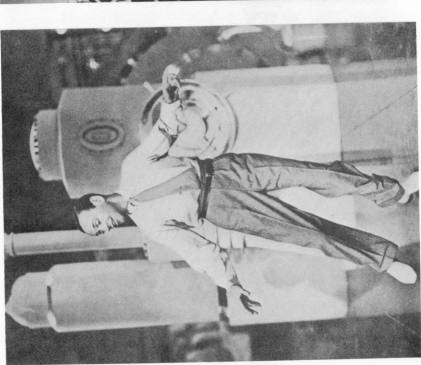

Movies and the dance. What the movies can do

its whole sophomore class reading and rereading *A Tale of Two Cities* before the picture came to town, selecting the scenes they thought would be filmed and discussing the changes it would be necessary to make in putting them on the screen. The Cleveland Public Library reports that when *David Copperfield* was about to appear on the local screen the demand for the book was so great that they bought 132 new copies. That brought their total up to 550 and before, during, and after the run of the film the shelves were bare. Cleveland's 51 copies of *Les Misérables* had been growing dusty but when the film came to the city they went into steady circulation. The same thing happened with the 40 copies of *The Count of Monte Cristo*, the 83 of Somerset Maugham's *Of Human Bondage*. The story repeats itself for book after book and city after city. One cites Cleveland only because the librarians there have been pioneers in taking the movie into partnership and because they are zealous and interested in compiling figures.

And the library is not by any means the whole measure of the movies' power. Films can make people not only read books but actually buy them. Look over the book counter at Woolworth's or in any drugstore. There beside Popeye and Mickey Mouse and Snow White are editions of *Tom Sawyer*, *The Prince and the Pauper*, *Treasure Island*, *Kidnapped*, *Captains Courageous*, with new "classics" added as they are screened. Publishers of both high- and low-priced editions find it good business to learn what standard books are being filmed and to issue reprints, illustrated more often than not with stills from the picture. Publishers of higher-priced editions engage in the same practice. Random House prepared a special *Romeo and Juliet* with comments by Norma Shearer ("Juliet") and Professor William Strunk, academic adviser in the production of the film. Dodd, Mead published a film-illustrated edition of Shaw's *Pygmalion*. While *The Life of Emile Zola* was in the theaters Doubleday, Doran reissued Matthew Josephson's *Zola and His Times*, the Three Suns Press got out a special edition of *Nana*, and Consolidated Book Publishers issued two editions of *Nana*, one a replica of the original Paris first.

Another "first" was issued by Twentieth Century-Fox when they produced *Jesse James*, a replica of the first dime novel in the famous series. The only variant was the back cover which carried a pictorial advertisement for the film. Some thousands of copies were struck off. The publicity department planned to use them as an amusing way of calling the picture to the attention of editors, critics, and such folk, but the public insisted on buying the dime novel in large quantities. An edition of 500,000 was exhausted in no time and another half million had to be printed.

Is there any sort of book the movies cannot sell? *Snow White*, in editions ranging in price from 10¢

to $2.50, sold more than 20,000,000 copies. The film première of *The Good Earth* shot the sales of that book up to 3,000 a week. More copies of *Wuthering Heights* have been sold since the novel was screened than in all the previous ninety-two years of its existence, and this despite its steady presence on the required reading lists of school and college classes. Whatever its services to literature, the cinema can certainly maintain that it is an ally of the publishing trade.

The ally is not only powerful but brave, for the producer who films a classic walks among spears. The eighty-five million Americans who go to the movies weekly are very jealous for the integrity of masterpieces. As one of the National Board of Review's "Young Reviewers" put it: "When a picture changes the idea of a book I think it is an insult to the author. Seems like when an author writes a classic and it lives through the ages it's presuming to change his plots and ideas." That attitude is almost universal. John Dugan, film critic of the *New Masses*, tells (July 5, 1938) a tale of a taxi driver whom he found reading Stevenson's *Kidnapped*.

He was scowling. We expressed interest in his literary bent. "I'm just checking up on that movie called *Kidnapped*," he said. "Those (unprintable term) changed it all around from the book. There ain't no girl in the book and this David Balfour was a lot older than Freddie Bartholomew." He described the other deviations taken by Daryl Zanuck. My friend's charges were completely documented. He was an angry consumer. "I've been checking on these guys ever since I read *Rebecca of Sunnybrook Farm* and then went to see the movie. Jeez, what a gyp that was." We agreed. "Why, if I had any dough I'd sue Zanuck for fraud!" he said. "They have no right to put over stuff like that on the public."

The producers are acutely aware of this state of mind. They are more concerned to satisfy it than to please the critics who dilate on the difference between a novel and a film. David Selznick has made an interesting pronouncement on the subject:

"I don't believe in reconstructing a story. I believe, if there are faults in construction, it is better to keep them than to try to change them around, because no one can certainly pick out the chemicals which contribute to the making of a classic. And there is always the danger that, by tampering, you may destroy the essential chemical."

This is a perfectly logical state of mind in an industry which, as we have seen, walks in fear of the grapevine, believes in cycles but thinks them unpredictable, and credits its most spectacular achievements to hunches.

The biggest job [Mr. Selznick continues] in adapting a well-beloved work is that of getting it down to the length of a feature film. And I have discovered that the public will forgive you for any number of omissions—particularly of subordinate material which is not directly connected with the main plot—but it won't forgive you for deliberate changes. For that reason I have found it best to make the bridging scenes which span the omissions as suggestive as possible. That is, by picking up dialogue and even phrases from other parts of the book and using such to construct the bridging scenes, the audience is given the illusion of seeing and hearing that with which they are already familiar.

Even when the book to be filmed is not a classic hallowed by time but only a best seller of the moment this attitude of Mr. Selznick's is the safest for a producer to take. The comparison of book and picture is for a vast audience the beginning of film criticism. It is the point, probably, at which teachers of motion picture appreciation might most profitably go to work.

The literary classics have certainly no reason to regard the movie as a vampire; in the case of the best seller there seems to be a fairly even division of assistance. The producers make their purchases among the book successes of the year not so much because of their adaptability for films—they have bought up *How to Win Friends and Influence People*—as because a large amount of national advertising of the title has already been done. On the other hand, the filming of a book means not only large emoluments for screen rights to the author but also increased sales. The American Institute of Public Opinion has demonstrated strikingly the influence of the movies upon the country's reading. In 1937 and again in 1938 the Institute took a survey through a cross section of the population from New England to California, asking share croppers, professors, housewives, telephone girls, business men, farmers, people working for the WPA, "What is the most interesting book you have ever read?" The answers, tabulated, ran like this:

1937

The Bible
Gone with the Wind
Anthony Adverse
The Good Earth
Magnificent Obsession
The Green Light
Les Misérables
Ben Hur
David Copperfield
The Count of Monte Cristo
Little Women
Drums Along the Mohawk
American Doctor's Odyssey
Treasure Island
How to Win Friends and Influence People
Uncle Tom's Cabin
All Quiet on the Western Front
The Virginian
Adventures of Tom Sawyer

1938

The Bible
Gone with the Wind
Anthony Adverse
The Citadel
How to Win Friends and Influence People
The Good Earth
Ben Hur
Northwest Passage
Little Women
A Tale of Two Cities
Les Misérables
Magnificent Obsession
Adventures of Tom Sawyer
Treasure Island
The Count of Monte Cristo
Robinson Crusoe
Ivanhoe
The Green Light
David Copperfield
Call of the Wild

One thing comes immediately to my mind about the leading books in the list [says George Gallup, director of the Institute, in the *New York Times Book Review* of January 15, 1939]. Nearly all of them have been seized upon by Hollywood as motion picture material. Even the Bible has been screened in part. *Anthony Adverse* was brought to the screen and became one of the leading "money" films of 1935. *The Citadel, The Good Earth, Little Women* and *A Tale of Two Cities* have recently been turned into outstanding pictures. Hollywood is preparing to produce a film version of Kenneth Roberts' *Northwest Passage* and has even scooped up the title rights to Dale Carnegie's personality handbook, *How to Win Friends and Influence People. Ben Hur*, seventh on the list, is not among the books filmed recently but it was one of the greatest box-office pictures of all time.

What film treatment may mean to the life of a book is indicated by the fact that merely to break even a good picture has to show to about 15,000,000 persons. A book, on the other hand, can become a best seller if it sells a few thousand copies. Hollywood did not create the original popularity of these books, but in giving them film treatment and a far greater audience the movies have unquestionably added to the circulation and endurance of the books themselves.

Though the films, with rare exceptions, are made from novels the influence of the movies upon books is by no means confined to fiction. They are great promoters also of collateral reading. The appearance in town, for instance, of *Lives of a Bengal Lancer* will sweep public library shelves of every book on India. *Marie Antoinette* creates a hunger for historical knowledge; so do *Suez* and *Marco Polo* and *Union Pacific. The Barretts of Wimpole Street* emptied Cleveland shelves for months not only of every life of the Brownings but of every copy of the poems of Elizabeth Barrett and the poems of Robert Browning. More than fifteen hundred libraries in different parts of the country are

taking advantage of these recurrent bursts of public curiosity by means of an ingenious device

"Union Pacific"

"The great Pacific railway,
For California hail!
Bring on the locomotive,
Lay down the iron rail!"

The Epic of Railroad
Pioneering in the West
Pictured in Books Chosen by
THE
Cleveland Public Library

THE UNION PACIFIC
In Fact
Building the Pacific Rail-
way; by Sabin
History of the Union Pacific;
by Trottman

In Fiction
The U. P. Trail; by Grey
Trouble Shooter; by Haycox
Mountain Divide;
by Spearman

"TRAILS, RAILS AND
WAR"

The Pony Express Goes
Through; by Driggs
Treasure Express: Epic Days
of the Wells-Fargo;
by Wilson
Trails, Rails and War;
by Perkins
They Built the West;
by Quiett

STORIES OF RAILROADS

Railroad West; by Meigs
Empire Builders; by Lynde
Hill Country; by Benson
The Empire Builder;
by Sullivan
The Wind Blew West;
by Lanham

Printed Through The
Courtesy Of
Loew's State
Presenting
CECIL B. DeMILLE's
"UNION PACIFIC"
Starring
BARBARA STANWYCK
JOEL McCREA
Loew's STATE
Starts FRI., May 5

worked out by the enterprising Cleveland Public
Library. In 1923 Cleveland launched its first
"bookmark," a wide strip of stiff paper inserted

for a week or so in every book circulated by the Library. The bookmark bears the title of a film

"WUTHERING HEIGHTS"

A tragic romance on the wild moors of northern England.

Books Suggested by the Story

Cleveland Public Library

ROMANCES IN THE GRAND MANNER

Wuthering Heights;
   by Emily Brontë
Bride of Lammermoor;
   by Scott
Jane Eyre;
   by Charlotte Brontë
Lorna Doone; by Blackmore
Castle of Otranto;
   by Horace Walpole

THE TRAGIC BRONTËS

They Lived;
   by Thornton-Cook
The Brontë Sisters;
   by Dimnet
Life of Charlotte Brontë;
   by Gaskell
The Three Brontës;
   by Sinclair
Wild Decembers, a Play;
   by Dane
Three Virgins of Haworth;
   by Romieu
Divide the Desolation;
   by MacFarlane

Printed Through The Courtesy Of
**Loew's
State Theatre**
Presenting
Samuel Goldwyn's
"WUTHERING HEIGHTS"
Co-Starring
MERLE OBERON
LAURENCE OLIVIER
DAVID NIVEN
At
Loew's STATE
Starts FRI., Apr. 28

currently showing in one of the local theaters and suggests interesting books to read before or after you see it.

The quick eye of the Hays Community Service Department marked the possibilities here. They spread the bookmark idea from Cleveland to other cities. Librarians adopted it eagerly; it increases circulation appreciably and the cost to the library is nil, for the theater where the selected film is showing is only too happy to pay the printing bill. Bookmarks now circulate in fifteen hundred libraries.

Encouraged by the success of the bookmarks and genuinely enthusiastic about the movies the Cleveland Library went on to other inventions. They publish a little periodical, *Books and Films*, listing pictures which "merit library coöperation" with suggestions to librarians on how to coöperate. They arrange display placards with stills from the picture, information about the book from which the film is drawn, and a shelf of books acquaintance with which will make seeing the movie more interesting. The *Library Journal*, national organ of the profession, now publishes suggestions for displays of this kind; the material is furnished by the Hays office and requests for it total in some cases as many as four thousand. So much enthusiasm does Cleveland stimulate for filmed books that even the Braille copies of *The Good Earth* were in constant use while the film was showing in a local theater!

The idea of making the library a source of telephone information about films playing in local theaters, originated in Macon, Georgia, was copied by the public library in Los Angeles, and is now nation wide. A call to the library in almost any city will give you not only the names of all the films showing in local playhouses but information about cast, director, suitability for youthful audiences, book source, or historical period.

It is difficult in the face of such evidence as this to deny to the motion picture the power of making people read, but the skeptics who feared first that the movies would stop all reading and then that they would present films as substitutes for the literary classics have now another anxiety: aren't the movies vitiating literary taste, creating the impression that the filming, and consequent popularizing, of *any* book is a service to letters? Confusion is worse confounded, the skeptics insist, by the fact that *If I Were King* may very well make a better movie than *A Midsummer Night's Dream*, that *Mutiny on the Bounty* is probably more exciting on the screen than *Les Misérables*. Is Metro-Goldwyn-Mayer, they ask, really doing a service to Shakespeare by offering a trip to Stratford-on-Avon to the girl who makes the best scrapbook of stills from *Romeo and Juliet?* What impression of the process of poetic creation will the schoolboy get who sees Rudyard Kipling riding out to battle with the British troops in *Gunga Din* and then turning off a poem by candlelight in his tent as though it were part of the day's newspaper assignment? There is already on record one college freshman who cited this sequence to his instructor as a refutation of Wordsworth's theory of poetry as emotion recollected in tranquillity. Who will set right the Motion Picture Appreciation Clubs who think they are contributing to culture by promoting the discussion of such filmed novels as those of Lloyd Douglas or Anthony Hope? A club in Massachusetts, for instance, reports proudly in a nationally circulated bulletin that

due to recent world events *The Prisoner of Zenda* stimulated unusual interest. Discussion about the social attitudes involved in the picture finally reached a culmination when various members debated, pro and con, the contrast of Flavia with the Duchess of Windsor: "If England had needed Edward as much as Flavia's country needed her, would Mrs. Simpson have been willing to sacrifice her love for honor and patriotism?" was one of the questions. Elizabeth, who had not only prepared a report on the novel, *The Prisoner of Zenda*, but had also told the club members the sequel story, *Rupert of Hentzau*, thought that Flavia was more patriotic than Mrs. Simpson.

In another issue of the same organ a university dean draws from the film of *The Prince and the Pauper* a "lesson of identity in moral standards":

Both rich and poor steal, murder, and are cruel for the sake of their own selfish goals. The methods are different, but there is no distinction in fundamental principles. Greatness has no guarantee of goodness.

Possessions do not stimulate generosity. Education carries no assurance of justice. Formal religion does not generate mercy and kindness. Materialism destroys in every walk of life the fundamental ideals of neighborliness.

If the movies are teaching the millions to think about literature in such terms as these are they doing her a service, the skeptics ask.

Suppose, on the other hand, they continue, you film a really immortal masterpiece, will not the screen version of the novel or play have all the shortcomings of an illustrated edition and more besides? What the reader receives first in an illustrated book is not the author's conception of a character but the artist's. The more striking the drawing, the more difficult it is to refocus the impression. The moviegoer introduced to a literary masterpiece by the screen finds himself too often in the position of the college student who bewildered his Shakespeare professor with a paper describing Mercutio as an aged roué. He had first met Mercutio on the screen, played by John Barrymore.

Against such diatribes as these the Better Film Councils and their ilk present the testimony of young people for whom the movies have brought to life plays or stories too complex for them to realize by their unaided imagination. For the unpracticed playgoer to visualize stage action as he reads is difficult, especially if he has only the haziest conception of the dress of a sixteenth- or an eighteenth-century gallant, the technique of a duel, or the rhythms of spoken verse. Most of these things, of course, a good teacher can provide, but one cannot always read with a good teacher at one's elbow. The sight of characters in their habits as they lived, moving and speaking like human beings, will often, it is argued, illuminate a whole body of literature which has lain confused and dark in a youthful mind.

Some testimonials to this power of the movies have been recorded by the National Board of Review's group of Young Reviewers. New York children, selected for the Board by their schools, preview films and report on them to their contemporaries all over the country. After the picture has been run off in the company's New York projection room the children discuss it, one of their number presiding, with that amazing combination of naïveté and poise characteristic of the modern school child. The only older person present sits unremarked in the background taking stenographic notes.

"I could place the characters so easy in this picture," said a boy of fifteen, for instance, of *Romeo and Juliet*, "and it was connected all the way through. When I read *Julius Caesar* last year I had to keep turning back to see who were his friends and who were his enemies—it was an awful job." A girl of fifteen: "I felt like I was really in the fifteenth century or Shakespeare's time or whenever it was." A girl of thirteen: "I understand the whole thing so much better now that I have seen the picture than I did when I read the play." And this is a single instance out of many. The case for the motion picture as a helpful ally of literature may not yet rest but literature and the theater must be at least constrained to admit the movies' good intentions.

Quite without intention the movies have influenced them also at another point, in technique. The contemporary theater is indebted to the cinema for some of its experiments with scenes on different levels, sudden black outs, spotlights that select now one group of characters and now another on a complex stage. By a variety of mechanical and lighting devices the stage is trying the feasibility and the advisability of adding to its own armory some of the most effective weapons of the screen: its swiftness of attack, its sudden contrasts, its ability to concentrate attention where it wants it, its power to batter the emotions from two or three directions at the same time. And experiment, even when it is not successful, is refreshing to any art.

More difficult to mark because of the subtle individual modifications they undergo are the motion picture influences on the written word. Certainly one is aware of them in the sharp successive pictures unrolling with cinematic swiftness in innu-

merable modern poems and novels, in the tendency
of the short story to become a picture or series of
pictures, in the current practice of describing action
or background in the manner of the scenario. John
Dos Passos, for instance, sets chronology and mood
in his novels by rapid-fire paragraphs, made up of
captions, headlines, and popular songs, which he
calls "Newsreels." Even more striking are the
chapter openings in Virginia Woolf's *The Years*
which read like poems and at the same time like
shooting scripts. They make one wonder whether
a technique of script writing for publication may
not one day be developed, something akin to the
descriptions of rooms and characters in Shaw's
published plays. H. G. Wells, that dweller in the
future, has already written a novel, *The King Who
Was a King*, in the form of a scenario. It is not a
very good novel but it was written in 1929 before
the days of sound. He could do something better
now and he probably will or at least he will have
emulators. Actual scripts of screen plays are being
brought out in book form by established publishing houses and the practice seems to be on the increase. A collection of the *Foremost Films of 1938*
has been issued and the editor, Frank Vreeland,
intends to make it an annual affair like the O'Brien
collections of short stories. The ten "best" films of
the year, selected on the basis of critics' approval,
trade paper comments, popularity with the public,
and elements of interest to college students of the

cinema, are presented in five-thousand-word summaries condensed from the shooting scripts.

Compared to its influence on literature the services of the screen to the plastic arts are not as yet considerable. The industry itself is convinced that it has trained the eyes of millions by showing them night after night series of well-arranged pictures. They are certain that anyone who goes often to the movies must have unconsciously acquired some knowledge of the elements of composition. They point with pride, for instance, to the fact that Cecil DeMille has attached to his staff an artist whose duty it is to "visualize" scenes in his productions, to compose groups and figures, arrange backgrounds and masses, offer suggestions for lighting to electricians and cameramen, make sketches from which the director can work. Mr. DeMille was moved to engage his artist, Dan Sayre Groesbeck, when he saw the 6,400-foot-square mural, said to be the largest in the world, he painted for the Santa Barbara Courthouse.

Not all directors of course work in this way; most of them prefer to "visualize" for themselves, but very many of them produce beautifully composed scenes and though the effect on the artistic standards of the audience would be difficult to estimate, even by a Gallup poll, that they should make some impression is certainly not beyond the bounds of possibility. Whether technicolor will prove educational in the same way is a question for the still more distant future. Eventually we must probably expect to see all our pictures in color but that may mean either a sharpening or a blurring of the color sense of the nation. Technicolor is still in a primitive state. Only its most earnest students are aware that it ought not to be used casually, as it is now generally used, merely to heighten reality by reproducing the tints of nature. Actually, the experts say, technicolor in regulating the emotion in a scene, in making contrasts and climaxes, has a power even greater than that of the camera, and, like music, color, if not skillfully regulated, may work clean contrary to the photographic effects. Certainly many of the things that are now being done with color are bad for the artistic taste of the eighty-five million. The best opportunity the public has at present to feel the artistic possibilities of color on the screen is in the Silly Symphonies and colored Mickey Mouse cartoons where Walt Disney is constantly making important aesthetic and technical experiments. Here again the movies are interesting their audience on two different levels. A Disney spectator always enjoys himself thoroughly. He is not troubled at all by the fact that what is going on is "significant" as well as amusing. He was not worried by the fact that *Wynken, Blynken and Nod* was not only a delight but a demonstration, which may well prove historic, of the possibility of making color into a plot. In the Disney cartoons, too, and in some of the others, the fusion of motion, color, and sound has reached a point of excellence which is far beyond anything yet attained by the feature film.

Of course now while they are enjoying Disney the eighty-five million are aware that he is officially "art." A celluloid painting of the vultures eying *Snow White's* wicked queen now hangs in the Metropolitan Museum. Private collectors, too, own Disneys. Scenes from *Snow White*, selected for preservation from the thousands made for the cartoon, have been eagerly bought.

Another gesture of coöperation between the arts was made by the Filmarte Theater in New York when it exhibited Renoir paintings in its lounge while *Grand Illusion*, directed by Pierre Renoir's son Jean, was showing in its auditorium. The fact that all three of the artist's sons are working, in different capacities, in the cinema is not without significance.

The most direct action of the screen in the assistance of art was made in England by Alexander Korda, but American exhibitors helped to circulate it widely. Charles Laughton's biographical study of *Rembrandt*, which Korda directed, undoubtedly brought the master's works to the attention of a great many people who had never heard of them or for whom they had no real vitality. It missed most of its opportunities, though, for teaching "art appreciation." As a piece of criticism or even as the biography of an artist the film was little more than a well-intentioned failure. Laughton of course made Rembrandt an individual but why his paintings shocked his contemporaries is barely suggested and why he felt constrained to paint as he did is never explained. Still the picture made clear what a scenarist with critical as well as biographical and narrative ideas might do to spread a knowledge of painters and their work.

Of all the arts music has promise of the most fruitful relations with the film. Annoyingly overinsistent as it frequently is, a musical accompaniment of some kind is almost essential to a picture. It gives the spectator a release, somewhat akin to physical action, without which the tense excitement of many scenes could not be borne. It intensifies emotion but makes it endurable. More than this it sets the tone of a scene or stresses it. Skillfully used, it can be almost as important as the script. Not all film scores today are made by combining Debussy, Mendelssohn, and the "Ride of the Valkyrie." Musicals like *Alexander's Ragtime Band*, *The Castles*, *Rose of Washington Square* revive nostalgically the song and dance tunes of a recent past. More significant is the use of American folk music in the background score of pictures which have nothing to do with singing or dancing. The large-scale Western *Stagecoach* set a precedent which will probably be developed further. The musical director, Boris Morros, keyed his score, as the costumes and properties were keyed, to the 1885 setting. He found his themes in the popular songs of the period, old love songs like "Lilly Dale" and "Rosa Lee," narrative ballads like "Joe the Wrangler," Stephen Foster's "Gentle Annie," that cowboy classic "The Trail to Mexico," and Owen Wister's "Ten Thousand Cattle."

Much fine original composition is being done to accompany scripts, and the names that figure on the screen are the same names that occur on concert programs of modern music: Hindemith, George Antheil, Erich Korngold, Russell Bennett, Werner Janssen, Max Steiner, Marc Blitzstein, Virgil Thomson, Aaron Copland, to mention only a few. Contemporary music, like all the other American arts, is seriously concerned to relate itself to a wide and popular audience. The concert hall seems to many composers too narrow a room for the things they want to say. To music in the cinema people listen at ease and naturally. It becomes an intimate part of their experience. When a composer wants to speak to a wide audience, when he wants to relate his music to currents in contemporary life, he finds today, better than in the theater or the ballet, his opportunity in the cinema. The work of course is specialized, difficult, and exacting. Not all musicians would find it possible to conform to its curious and rigid mechanical necessities, but those who care to apparently discover rich rewards.

A similar desire to be in the current of the present is bringing to Hollywood some important

performing musicians and a few well-known
though scarcely great conductors. Stokowski has
announced his desire to "bring the greatest music
to the greatest number of people." Walter Dam-
rosch is rounding off a long life of popularizing
great music on the concert platform by enlisting
the popularizing aid of the cinema. Those two may
be unusually eager for publicity but Paderewski
himself consented to play in a movie and so
did Heifetz. Alexander Brailowsky, Alfred Cortot,
Gregor Piatigorsky, and Jacques Thibaud are reported to be under contract. Opera singers of every
degree of eminence seem eager to get to Hollywood. There are material as well as spiritual rewards. Whenever a musician appears in a picture,
it is credibly alleged, not only does attendance at
his recitals increase decisively but the royalties on
his phonograph recordings mount to gratifying
proportions. It seems probable that the day is not
far distant when a soprano setting out on a concert
tour will think it more important to write after
her name "of MGM" or "of Paramount" than "of
the Metropolitan Opera."

It is difficult to separate movie and radio influence here but certainly movie influence is strong
though the singers who can take advantage of it
are fewer. They must be slender enough, or dashing enough, according to sex, to satisfy an audience
who are accustomed to the very best in glamour and
do not expect to be asked to use their imaginations

to reduce their heroes to correct proportions as an opera audience is trained to do.

As in the case of the best-selling novel, the movie which screens a nationally famous musician is taking advantage and giving it with the same hand. Asked why he signed Jascha Heifetz for *They Shall Have Music*, Goldwyn replied: "He's the greatest property in the show world today." He added that at least half a million people, out of that difficult twenty-six million who do not go regularly to the movies, will make a point of seeing a picture in which Heifetz plays. This seems not improbable when one remembers the appreciable number of non-moviegoing "intellectuals" who went to see the *Big Broadcast of 1938* because of a singularly detached incident in which Kirsten Flagstad suddenly appeared upon a rock and, for no apparent reason, began to sing "The Cry of the Valkyrie."

The headline concert stars do not monopolize the ministrations of the motion picture to music. The movies also encourage the minor musician, though it did look for a time as though the vampires were going to destroy him entirely. It was becoming the practice for a director to decide that he needed slow music here, a chase there, a plaintive solo violin, a triumphal chorus—and then to send down to the sound laboratory for so many feet of each. The big battle scene or the sunset or the terrible suspense that was recorded for a picture two years ago was just as useful, in slightly different proportions, for today's film. Gradually all the stock bits in the "public domain"—music on which the copyright has expired—the Beethoven and Wagner and Tschaikowsky and Gounod, were accumulating in tins and, except when a brand new score was composed for a film, there was very little for the musicians to do. Every time an orchestra put a new bit of a classic onto celluloid it was doing itself out of a job next winter. The musicians became desperate, and militant. If the producers wanted musicians ever, at all, they must make it possible for those musicians to eat and to keep in practice by exercising their skill. The American Federation of Musicians and the producers met and came to an agreement. The transferring or "dubbing" of sound tracks from old films to new has been stopped, except in certain special cases such as newsreels where speed of completion is essential. Each feature film must now have its sound made to fit. The plan, the Federation thinks, will increase the annual income of musicians by some $800,000, which can, if you like, be regarded as a contribution of the film to music.

The industry itself reckons its contributions to music in far less material terms. They pride themselves that they are advancing American taste by presenting classical music to the eighty-five million just as they are promoting culture by stimulating the reading of the literary classics. They point to the fact that, although they have not yet exercised it so widely, they have the same power to sell music that they have to sell books. Schirmer had to issue, for instance, a new popular edition of Gounod's "Ah! je veux vivre" after Deanna Durbin had sung it in *That Certain Age*. But just as some skeptics view with alarm the indiscriminate mass of printed matter which is presented to the moviegoer as "literature," so some musicians, even those most interested in music for the masses, listen with dismay to the so-called musical films. That form of presenting music, they point out, is all too similar to the current tendency to popularize science and philosophy by writing biographies of philosophers and scientists. The listener gets an impression that he understands something about which he knows really nothing of any importance. The mannerisms of a conductor, the inspired way he throws back his head, the graceful waving of his hands, are not, after all, the essential elements in a symphony. How far does a hypothetical familiarity with the love life of Beethoven contribute to one's understanding of the *Appassionata?* Does a closeup of the violinist's bow hand help you to interpret the César Franck sonata? And what impression can you get of a great work of music when it must be broken up into fragments for the convenience of the plot? These are surely legitimate questions but when so prominent a musician as Stokowski lends himself to closeups of picturesque conducting poses and makes no objection to directing symphonic snippets of great, alternating with near-great, works, it does not seem quite fair to blame the cinema for musical naïveté.

The cinema thinks also that it is contributing to culture by recording performances by great artists of the strings or piano. Closeups of expert technique are useful, it is said, to music students. That is possible, say the skeptics, but certainly their chief result is the fixing of the popular mind, where it is all too prone to fix itself, on virtuosity rather than on music. Still more dubious is the often-cited opportunity of studying at close range the lip and throat movements of singers, which is supposed to be one of the benefits the films confer upon aspiring students of voice. The eager modelers of themselves upon the great should be informed, the skeptics think, that the diva usually records her sound track separately so that in front of the camera she may sing *sotto voce* with her mind not on how she sounds but on how she looks. Attempts to imitate her photographed technique may have some curious vocal results.

One excellent elementary teaching device has been discovered in the filming of orchestras: as the theme passes from violins to oboes, to cellos, the camera moves with it picking up the different instruments as they pick up the theme. This is logical and often helpful but when the matter becomes more complex what is the camera to do? It must, if it is to hold the attention of a movie audience, keep on moving. If there is a plot behind the music the lens may focus upon some individual musician in whom we are supposed to be interested and show us his emotions while he plays, or it may swing to a special listener in the audience, or spread out to impress us with the importance of the occasion by showing us the whole auditorium. Then of course we forget the music as music. It becomes a sound background to a story. When there isn't any story the camera movement becomes painfully disturbing.

An experiment is now being made with plotless symphonic shorts, complete musical compositions played by a good orchestra as they would be played at a concert. The Overture to *Tannhäuser* and Schubert's *Unfinished Symphony* have been made so far. The orchestra is excellent, the recording good, but the camera troubles everybody. It moves about from instrument to instrument, from individual to group and group to individual; it backs away and takes in the whole orchestra; it comes close and shows the conductor's baton. The pictures are meaningless and the rhythm of the camera's motion is distractingly different from the rhythms of the music. The spectator with the faintest musical sense is made acutely uncomfortable or driven to close his eyes and try to confine his sensations to those of listening to a good phonograph. Another experiment is the color symphony in which bands of blue and purple and gold expand and contract and dance upon the screen, "interpreting" the playing of an unseen orchestra. There is at least the possibility here of a fusion of sense impressions such as one gets in ballet or opera. Disney seems to be trying something of this kind in the Musical Fantasia on which he is at work. It is possible, too, that the musical movie may develop someday into a really interesting form. So far the plots have been singularly dull, with songs, classic or popular, pulled in by the heels, but there seems to be no reason why a really lovely combination might not be achieved of picture, dance, and singing. We have had already some remarkable dance moments, though the music is not distinguished, in the Astaire and Rogers' pictures. The "revues" and "broadcasts" and "follies," just about the time they began to go out of fashion, were developing dances planned for the camera, interesting patterns, seen from a distance or from above, effects in black and white. The screen can certainly be of use to the art of the dance if the dance cares to have its help.

A word which recurs constantly when one is discussing the film and the other arts is radio. Actually of course radio is not an art at all but a transmitter of art like the phonograph. It touches the cinema really not on the artistic but on the industrial plane. And on the industrial plane the movie brings vampire charges against the radio. Movie talent is now the principal source upon which radio

draws for its programs. Since 1937 90 per cent of
the sponsored national radio programs have gone
out from Hollywood where one broadcaster after
another has set up a million-dollar plant in the
shadow of the film studios. There is scarcely a
screen name of any importance which does not figure as a "guest star" on some radio program. Sometimes radio popularity has brought a singer a
Hollywood contract. More often it is the other
way about. Tyrone Power who began in radio at $12
a week went up to $1,000 after the movies had
presented him to the nation. Even those who do not
command $10,000 weekly like Eddie Cantor, find
radio a very pleasant addition to income. Radio
appearances may be a good thing for a screen actor's prestige and his personal pocketbook but how
about their effect on his box-office? For a long
while the movie people were noncommittal on that
point. Producers not only permitted their stars to
be heard on sponsored programs but began to experiment with the arrangement of big programs
of their own. Finally, however, they came to a definite conclusion. Martin Quigley, whose *Motion
Picture Herald* is to the industry what the London
Times is to the British Cabinet, stated flatly, on
December 17, 1938, that "radio it not an ally. It is
a competitor of formidable proportions." Encouraged by this, exhibitors began to show specifically
how radio cut into their box-office receipts. They

reported that when an important star could on a certain night be seen on their screen and heard over the air on a radio hour, movie fans stayed at home and listened instead of coming to the theater. Daryl Zanuck of Twentieth Century-Fox fired the first gun in the now declared war by ordering Tyrone Power out of the Woodbury Soap program. Metro-Goldwyn-Mayer followed suit. Then other objections were voiced. Stars began to complain that their public personalities were damaged by the poor quality of the material they were given to broadcast. Publicity men had been growling for some time over the irresponsible chattering of radio "gossipers" who try to impress the public with their inside knowledge by slandering screen personalities.

Today a word more formidable than radio is occupying the attention of the industry—television. The correct current movie attitude towards television is the complacent assurance that it is not a danger, just a new medium of transmission which can be utilized for the benefit of the screen. There is a kind of shrillness in the tone, however, which suggests whistling to keep up courage. In any case television, like radio, is not an art but a mechanism of communication. Any anxiety it may cause the movies is financial, not artistic. If it is possible to watch news and sporting events as they take place, the importance of the newsreel may be diminished. When you can turn on a film in your home as easily as you dial the radio, times may be hard for the theaters. Scenarist, actor, and director, however, will continue to flourish.

When, examining the complex and not very well-codified evidence in the relations of the movies to the other arts, one attempts to come to some sort of final conclusion, the main presumption is the extraordinarily heartening one that appetite grows by what it feeds on. The appetite may need to be refined but its mere existence would seem to be a cause of rejoicing; the more a man has of one art, apparently, the more he wants of others. It argues well, then, for the cultural future of America that eighty-five million people go to the movies every week.

The movies are not only creating a hunger for art, they are making art for millions of Americans a necessary and natural part of life. One of the charms of moviegoing is that it does not have to be planned in advance; there is no need to dress for the occasion or to arrive at a stated hour. There are few emotional experiences which can be enjoyed so much at the dictates of mood and honest desire. The dweller in New York City, to be sure, can usually go to a concert or a play whenever he really feels like it, but in the smaller community music and theater are "events," with all the attendant paraphernalia, sometimes pleasant, more often distracting. Only the movies are always there when you want them. Only the movies take it for granted that half the audience will arrive late and climb over the other half, who can retaliate by climbing out early. Only the movies permit a party to expand or contract on the way to the theater without complications or financial loss. And in consequence millions of people take their movies quite naturally, without the affectation or pretense that clouds the atmosphere of so many arts.

There is still another cultural contribution of the movies to American life which has not yet, I think, been sufficiently remarked. The movies are furnishing the nation with a common body of knowledge. What the classics once were in that respect, what the Bible once was, the cinema has become for the average man. Here are stories, names, phrases, points of view which are common national property. The man in Cedar Creek, Maine, and the man in Cedar Creek, Oregon, see the same movie in the same week. When they meet, at the convention in Chicago, they talk together easily because they speak the same language, the language of the Marx Brothers and Charlie McCarthy, of Mickey Mouse and Popeye and Carole Lombard. They understand each other's allusions and take each other's references as easily as the medieval travelers speaking Low Latin on the Elbe or the Rhine. The movies span geographic frontiers; they give the old something to talk about with the young; they crumble the barriers between people of different educations and different economic backgrounds. Perhaps this dominance of the motion picture is a cause for regret. The comparative beauty of the King James version, the poems of Ovid, and the scenarios of Frances Marion as cultural food for the race may be debatable, but there can be no question of the richness and pervasiveness of the common knowledge and there is no reason why its quality should not improve with age.

IX

"THE LURE OF PROPAGANDA"

MARCH 28, 1939, is a date of importance in American history. On that day the motion picture industry extended an official welcome to ideas. It was pronounced by Will H. Hays, President of the Motion Picture Producers and Distributors of America in his annual report to that organization. The reports of Mr. Hays are often significant social documents. As the official statements of attitude of the art most responsive to public taste they indicate sometimes important things about the movement of the American mind.

Before 1939 Mr. Hays was an inflexible champion of what he called "pure entertainment," entertainment unadulterated, unsullied by any infiltration of "propaganda." To take the weekly quarters of the eighty-five million on any other basis seemed to him a breach of faith. It is instructive to set side by side the propaganda sections of the Hays' reports for 1938 and 1939.

March 28, 1938

In a period in which propaganda has largely reduced the artistic and entertainment validity of the screen in many other countries, it is pleasant to report that American motion pictures continue to be free from any but the highest possible entertainment purpose. The industry has resisted and must continue to resist the lure of propaganda in that sinister sense persistently urged upon it by extremist groups. The function of the entertainment screen is to entertain, by whatever wholesome theme or treatment writers, artists and dramatists can create. There is no other criterion. Only those who have a selfish purpose to serve can cry out against such a policy.

The distinction between motion pictures with a message and self-serving propaganda is one determinable only through the process of common sense. Between the screen's basic function of entertainment and recreation for the millions which it must serve, and the art's higher purpose as an aesthetic, educational, and dramatic medium of first importance, there is room, much of which is still unused, for the presentation and treatment of the greatest theses of life, literature, music, and drama. But there is no place in motion pictures for self-serving propaganda.

Entertainment is the commodity for which the public pays at the box-office. Propaganda disguised as entertainment would be neither honest salesmanship nor honest showmanship.

The movie theatre can afford the soft impeachment that most pictures reflect no higher purpose than to entertain, with "escapist" entertainment if you please. If entertainment and recreation are what 85,000,000 people weekly seek in American motion picture theatres, and they do, so much the better for the screen and the universal public which it serves.

March 27, 1939.

The past year has been notable for the rising tide of discussion as to the social function of the screen. In a period of great tension in world affairs, the conflict of opinion, however, as between those who would preserve the motion picture theatre as a center of popular recreation and those who would emphasize the social import of the art was more often apparent than real. The increasing number of pictures produced by the industry which treat honestly and dramatically many current themes proves that there is nothing incompatible between the best interests of the box-office and the kind of entertainment that raises the level of audience appreciation whatever the subject treated.

None the less, the discussion that proceeds is the greatest possible tribute to the progress of the screen. For it is proof of the fact that an entertainment art for the millions has risen to such high estate that the best which the living theatre has been able to produce or which other artistry can create is now demanded from the films. It is not so long ago that thrilling action for its own sake was considered satisfying "movie"; that the custard pie was the symbol of hilarity and amusement from the screen; that the chase was sure-fire entertainment technique; that boy-meets-girl supplied all the drama that a motion picture audience apparently demanded.

Whatever may have been the merits or demerits of each picture from an artistic standpoint, today competent critics, in and out of the industry, are able to point to a succession of pictures which dramatized present-day social conditions, which exposed slum areas in many of our great cities, which placed in true perspective the problems of medicine and medical care, which dealt with issues of war and peace, which treated of crime and crime-breeding, which showed human beings struggling for individuality against the forces of an increasingly complex civilization, which discussed the values of our present-day democracy and emphasized the traditions that have made this nation great, which exposed racketeering, which treated of the problems of adolescence and which dealt with other themes notable for their educational value. . . .

The better-picture movement was inaugurated with the help of important public groups of nation-wide followings, which coöperated with the industry to help raise public demand in order to justify the supply of pictures of the better kind.

In this respect the industry itself invited the challenge which producers, writers, directors and artists must accept in order to raise ever higher the standards of the screen. That is why today so many demands are focused on the industry and why our studios must answer with the greatest possible variety of entertainment for a universal public.

Significant as the change is, from glory in "escapist entertainment" to glory in "pictures that dramatize present-day social conditions," this second report of Mr. Hays is not a battle cry, merely an official recognition of a force which had at last grown too strong to be ignored. For years it had been breaking spasmodically through the hard safe formula of excitement and escape, for years insistent voices had been urging that a far larger section of the eighty-five million than the producers suspected were interested in other things besides boy-meets-girl. The industry steadily gave them the lie but it was polite about it; it referred to the objectors always as the "class" audience or the "intellectuals," implying that their ideas are lofty though not necessarily sound, that what is wrong is not so much their principles as their mathematics. The industry could not deny, however, that from 1930 on these critical members of the motion picture audience have steadily increased in number. More and more intelligent comment on the film is being written and read, more and more people are going to the movies not just to relax or to pass the time but for the same reasons that take them to the theater. There are the "montage boys" interested primarily in the aesthetics of the screen; there are others whose concern is to have the movies pay some attention to the problems of real life; there are still others who are simply looking for entertainment a little more mature than spectacular musicals and goofy comedies. Their combined point of view was expressed by Archibald MacLeish writing in *Stage* (January, 1939) on "Propaganda vs. Hollywood."

The problem, he said, was

whether a form of art which ignored everything comprehended under the term "social issues" in this time could have vitality—could have the fourth dimension of life. More broadly it was the question whether a form of art, an action in art, which had no relation to the deepest emotions, the strongest convictions, the most characteristic experiences of the time, was not of necessity a kind of artistic and spiritual abortion incapable of life.

Hollywood is in trouble at the box-office. And the reason why Hollywood is in trouble at the box-office is precisely that its pictures lack the fourth dimension of life. And the reason its pictures lack the fourth dimension of life is precisely that they do not know their own time, do not present their own time, do not belong to their own time, and therefore, quite naturally, have lost the interest of their own time.

The Hays manifesto, coming a few months later, might almost be taken as a reply. In any event the industry has now admitted the possibility of making movies with "ideas," with "content," with "propaganda." The intellectuals have won their first point, but it now becomes apparent how many points there are, how complex, entangled, and difficult is the whole great problem of motion pictures and propaganda.

Certainly one of the most important of its tangled ramifications is the problem of the Government and motion picture propaganda. The Beards, in *America in Midpassage*, have shown in some detail how the Roosevelt administration saw the potential power of the movies and seized it for the support of the naval expansion policy of 1938. In an interesting section on the relations between government and entertainment they discuss the way our Government has made use of the movies. One might say with equal truth that the movies have made use of the Government.

It was, of course, wise of the industry to show a happy readiness to coöperate, to make a good impression upon the Government against a day of need. They felt the monopoly investigation coming afar off and they wanted all the good will they could build up. But even had good will been quite unnecessary it was to the movies' advantage to make *Submarine D-1*, *Navy Blue and Gold*, *Annapolis Salute*, *Wings over Honolulu*, *Men with Wings*, and the rest of them. The producers who were willing to coöperate with the Government, to take plot suggestions, to cut out pacifist speeches here and there, found at their disposal, quite free of charge, submarines, gunboats, airplanes; the very latest models, manned by experts. There are few objects which photograph in motion so well as boats and planes. Pictures in which they are the mainspring of the plot are almost certain to be exciting. There was no question that the movie audiences found the naval pictures thrilling. They found in them, too, the kind of information that delights Americans, information about how things work. Added to that the Government's pictures were romantic; the navy can always be counted on for a good love and honor conflict. The movies could say to themselves complacently that they were "keeping faith with their public," offering them "pure entertainment," exciting stories against a picturesque background. They were also keeping faith with their stockholders by reducing production costs. If the Government was getting what it wanted, fine, but so far as the movies and their public were concerned the propaganda was incidental.

About the Latin-American good will propaganda of 1938 and 1939 both the Government and Hollywood were more frank. The State Department openly invited coöperation in a projected million-dollar propaganda program to cement relations between the United States and the twenty Latin-American republics. The motion picture industry, drawing a distinction between "selfish propaganda" and "spreading information about the

American way of life," was delighted at the prospect of assistance in working the South American
market which it sees as the best substitute for its
dwindling European audience. The project en-
visages the production of films about the United
States for distribution in Latin America and a film
on Latin America for distribution here; the estab-
lishment of a film exchange; and the installation
of projection equipment in the larger American
embassies. That, of course, is no new idea. Several
United States embassies in Europe make extensive
use of American films.

Towards the Government making films for itself, not merely lending its equipment to Hollywood or helping them expand their markets, the
industry is inclined to look with a slightly suspicious eye. That is an attitude which it shares with
a great many United States citizens. It was not
until the critics began to talk with enthusiasm about
Pare Lorentz's film *The River* and audiences up
and down the nation were receiving it with applause that most people realized that making motion pictures was one of their Government's
regular activities. Small groups of citizens had long
been gratefully aware of the fact. Farmers' organizations, schools, churches, clubs had looked
with interest and profit at films prepared by the
Department of Agriculture, the Children's Bureau,
the Federal Housing Administration, or the Bureau
of Mines. Exceedingly valuable for their purpose

most of these films belong in the "educational" rather than the "entertainment" class. They are not designed for the regular movie theater but for showings in schools or private halls and they are circulated without charge. People look at them not so much because they want to be entertained as because they want to learn something.

When the average citizen thought about this movie making it seemed to him a perfectly legitimate Government activity, like publishing pamphlets for farmers on how to get rid of Japanese beetles or for housewives on the best ways of putting up tomatoes. It might be a little fancy to teach things like that by motion pictures but it was nothing to worry about. The average citizen had a different attitude when he found the Government using motion pictures as a means of reporting to its citizens on its activities or giving account of its use of their tax money. This, said the average citizen, is political propaganda; the Government is making an emotional appeal to us to approve what they have done and to elect them again. He knew quite well that movies delighted and excited him and he was suspicious that the Government was taking an unfair advantage in making this approach. He had read about propaganda films made by the Governments in Germany and Italy. Was this something of the same kind? And finally, whatever the motive, making movies is an extravagance.

The eighty-five million think of the process only in terms of Hollywood.

The Government replied that it is one of the important duties of the representatives of any democratic people to give accountings of their stewardship; that the American people had always expected and desired this; that Federal agencies had for years issued elaborate reports, had furnished information on their activities to magazines and newspapers, had sent speakers up and down the country to explain what they were doing. When radio became an important channel for telling Americans things they wanted to know the Government began to use radio. Now it was turning to that other great American medium of communication, the motion picture. Making films without star casts and elaborate sets and high-priced writers of dialogue is a comparatively inexpensive business. The Department of the Interior could make all the movies it wants to make in the next twenty years for the cost of the bow of one battleship. People are suspicious of the Government's use of the motion picture, says the Government, only because it is more effective than other media, easier to pay attention to, harder to disregard.

The first Government film that attracted critical attention, national and international, was *The Plow That Broke the Plains*. It tells the story of the dust bowl and the drought, our magnificent natural resources and how we squandered them by careless use, the resultant misery, and the suggested remedy. *The River*, an even better piece of film making, shows "how we took the Mississippi Valley apart" by frenzied cotton planting and reckless deforestation; it pictures the terrible result in floods; and then explains that "we have the power" to put the valley together again. The maker of these two pictures was Pare Lorentz, a movie critic who had made a serious study of the art of the cinema. His imagination was kindled by the dramatic qualities in a Department of the Interior report. The Farm Security Administration gave him a budget which by Hollywood standards was very small but otherwise he had a free hand. He was able to enlist, at a low cost because they too saw the project as exciting, the services of some of the best cameramen in the country, skilled musicians, artists, technicians.

Because *The Plow That Broke the Plains* was released during Roosevelt's second-term campaign the industry smelled political propaganda and kept away from it. *The River* appeared after election and it was an even better film. Paramount, as a gesture of coöperation and good will, agreed to circulate it as though it were one of the company's own shorts. This brought a theater audience of some tens of millions. The other Federal agencies cannot speak in such large figures but their audiences are big enough to be interesting. The De-

The United States Government makes reports to its citizens by means of films which any group may borrow without charge. Pare Lorentz's "The River," original and exciting in technique, dramatizes the cause and cure of floods. "Hands" shows the purpose of the WPA.

Problems of propaganda: What can an audience stand? Paul Muni's "I Am a Fugitive from a Chain Gang" exhausted spectators by the horror of its realism.

Problems of propaganda: What will an audience believe? Francis Lederer and Edward G. Robinson played "Confessions of a Nazi Spy" as a piece of patriotic service. Most spectators thought it just an exciting movie.

partment of Agriculture estimates that five million people see each of its films; the Department of the Interior reckons four million.

The Government makes its movies by three different methods. Some agencies engage technicians for each job, as was done with Lorentz. Some have their own laboratories and field camera units. Some have films produced for them under contract by commercial concerns. Some direct and distribute films financed by industry and commerce. A project for a centralized Federal film unit went down to destruction with the Federal Theater Project but the makers of Government movies look towards some form of centralized bureau as the ultimate system.

All the Government agencies make their films on both 35mm. and 16mm. stock so that they can be shown on either large or small projectors. They consider the films as the property of the nation and circulate them without charge except for expressage. They stipulate that no admission shall be charged at private showings though they are glad to have movie theaters include Government films as shorts in their regular programs. The film making agencies are sure that as they learn to make their pictures more and more interesting and entertaining an increasing number of theaters will take advantage of them and soon the eighty-five million will begin to watch for them on programs as they now look for *The March of Time*. The spirit in which the Government films are made has been succinctly described by Fanning Hearon, at that time Director of Motion Pictures in the Department of the Interior, in an exceedingly informative article (from which I have taken many of the preceding facts) in *The Journal of Educational Sociology* for November, 1938.

We make [he says] films of a broad educational nature with one purpose particularly in mind. This purpose is to be perfectly frank with the people about what the Government is doing with their money; and to fulfill the purpose we are making film documents—films of fact, films with nouns and verbs, but not adjectives. There is more human interest in Government than in any single subject on earth, so it is completely unnecessary to dress up a motion picture about it with superlatives. Let's just say "the Government is building a dam," not that "the great Government is building the biggest dam in the world."

The problem of the Government and motion pictures is curiously entangled with another ramification of the propaganda problem, the question of motion picture propaganda by big business. The entanglement comes because the Bureau of Mines makes a practice of circulating movies sponsored, which is to say financed, by private industry. The Bureau is careful to see that all direct advertising of products or trade-marks is eliminated from the films it circulates but, provided the picture is tech-

nically interesting, it makes no objection to the
more subtle "public relations" advertising, selling
to the public business and the economic theories
of business, which is the fundamental purpose of
most of these films.

There are other distributors of public relations
films, most important the "Guaranteed Distribution of Advertising Motion Pictures, Operated by
the Motion Picture Bureau of the YMCA for the
Benefit of American Industry." Makers of commercial films and the big advertising agencies also
act as distributors. In 1933 a 16mm. sound projector simple enough for an amateur to operate was
perfected, so was the "talking slide film" which
combines a sound track with slides something like
those of the old magic lantern. These made it possible for the big production companies to circulate
their films to churches, clubs, fraternal organizations, and above all colleges and schools, for business has been studying the propaganda techniques
of the dictators. In 1936 the executives of General
Motors meeting at White Sulphur Springs, were
told that

since 1929 nearly 17,000,000 young people have come
of age. What do they think of the ability of industry
to provide for their future? ... What is going to be
their verdict in the current conflict between individ-
ualism and the corporate state? If you are interested
in the part youth is playing in the modern world,
study the records of the dictators of Europe. Each

move is built around a proposal to give youth a place in the sun.

General Motors is an enthusiastic maker of public relations films; so are the National Association of Manufacturers, the United States Steel Corporation, and many others. Westinghouse, for instance, has a picture called *New Frontiers* which tries to prove to the public "that Westinghouse plays an important part in national economic life and also affects the lives of every individual in the country." *Golden Years of Progress*, made for the Chicago World's Fair by a group of advertising agencies, was designed to "bring home to the public what a force general advertising has been in giving them the standard of living existing today." General Motors' *Progress on Parade* was based on the theme: "Who Serves Progress Serves America." The United States Steel Corporation has a story of steel in technicolor with special emphasis on "the human side of steel," demonstrated by shots of the happy home life of steel workers. The National Association of Manufacturers sells to business men for distribution among their employees and their clientele a "Business Facts Program" composed of five films:

1. *The Light of a Nation* gives the story of American institutions ... and discusses the various "isms" which threaten the nation.

2. *Men and Machines* is a picturized answer to the argument that machines destroy jobs.

3. *Flood Tide* analyzes the present-day tax situation, warns against rising costs of government.

4. *The Constitution* points out what this remarkable document means to us and how it preserves our individual freedom and our freedom of enterprise.

5. *American Standards of Living* forcibly portrays what the American working man enjoys as the fruit of his labor under the American system.

An extended study of commercial propaganda films, to which I am indebted for these facts, was published in *Harper's Magazine*, February, 1938, by S. H. Walker and Paul Sklar, "Business Finds Its Voice, Part II, Motion Pictures and Combined Efforts."

How far should the Government go in propaganda for itself? How far should it go in helping the propaganda of important national groups? These are interesting questions but they have not been brought so sharply to the attention of the general public as the problem of the right of small groups to use the screen for the expression of their own ideas. When, for example, the sympathizers with Loyalist Spain produce a film which dramatically expounds the Loyalist cause, should the American friends of Franco ignore that film, boycott it, try to keep it off the screen, or answer it with a counter-propaganda film? All four methods have been tried and are being tried by both sides in the great controversies of the hour.

The small independent producing units that

sprang up and flourished through the 1930's were powerful among the factors that converted the screen to ideas. They are often hard put to it for funds but what they lack in money they make up by heavy endowments of talent, for they reckon among their numbers artists of the first rank in almost every field. They make films about Spain, about China, about Czecho-Slovakia, about the United States, not just newsreels but pictures with unity and ideas and techniques so original and beautiful that critics are filled with enthusiasm and audiences, not always small, are stirred to applause and tears. Most notable of their efforts so far have been Herbert Kline's *Crisis* taken in Prague, Joris Ivens' *Spanish Earth* which presented the case for the Loyalists, and his *The 400,000,000* which spoke for China. The Motion Picture Guild is now at work on a picture based on Erika Mann's *School for Barbarians* and Frontier Films is dramatizing the findings of the LaFollette Civil Liberties Committee.

Films carrying ideas straight counter to these have been made and are in the making by opposing groups. In March, 1939, Film Facts, Inc., issued *Spain in Arms*.

The Loyalist army is shown in its first uprisings against the government. Churches are burned, skeletons of nuns are dug up and left at the entrances of the ruined churches, the police are powerless and anti-Loyalists are executed. Meanwhile the Nationalists, under General Franco, have organized and Franco starts his march from the south.

"To defend the American Constitution from alien philosophies of Communism and Fascism" is the purpose of American Films Foundation, a non-profit organization listing among the members of its advisory board officers of the Military Training Camps Association, American Women Against Communism, the Clergy League of America, the Society of Mayflower Descendants, and the DAR. Their first film, *We, the People*, is about the Constitution; the second, *The Right to Work*, tells how necessary it is for capital and labor to work together.

It would be instructive if some organization like the Institute for Propaganda Analysis would screen on the same program some of these different attempts to arouse America with movies and would analyze the relations between the power of these films, their art, and their truth.

The occasional picture with an idea which the industry itself has produced has raised still other problems of propaganda. Is it, for instance, the function of the screen merely to present a situation or should it also suggest a remedy?

The causes which the industry has so far espoused are all causes in which "everybody" believes, causes like the desirability of safe driving, the importance of preventing crime, the beauties of peace, or the necessity for better housing. The promotion of these causes is not so often planned as the result of chance. The motion picture crusade against slums, for example, was instigated by the popularity of the "*Dead End* Kids." When the screen took over, softening it here and there, Sidney Kingsley's play of New York tenement children, they took with it the boy actors whose East Side lingo had delighted Broadway audiences and proceeded to delight the nation. *Dead End* was the biggest motion picture box-office success of the year. Immediately the screen went into a cycle of youthful toughness with tenement backgrounds. The "message" of most of these slum pictures was that bad housing breeds criminals; the suggested remedy, a little more understanding and charity on the part of the rich. Even when Paramount went so far as to film the Federal Theater's outspoken "*—one-third of a nation*" they managed to substitute an individual conversion for the government action recommended by the play. The intellectuals were encouraged by the beginnings of these films but not by their fade-outs.

One topic on which the producers have thought themselves really "daring" is the horrors of war. Though they are under the impression that it requires more courage than it does today to write yourself down a pacifist, they have filmed strong documents for peace, novels like Remarque's *All Quiet on the Western Front*, plays like *They Gave Him a Gun*. And while they filmed these, the industry kept on making big navy pictures. There is another propaganda problem there.

Another difficult problem was posed as long ago as 1932 when Warner Brothers made *I Am a Fugitive from a Chain Gang*, a dramatization of a case and a book then prominently before the public mind. A terrible indictment of the South's way with state's prisoners it was exciting, well directed, excellently acted—it starred Paul Muni, but it strengthened, if anything, the case for pure entertainment. The horror is too great and the horror of pictures is far more unnerving than the comparatively intellectual impact of horror from the printed word. The horror of realism, too, is a very different thing from the romantic blood and violence of pirate melodramas or large-scale Westerns or even gangster thrillers. Certainly people ought to be aware of the cruelties practiced on mankind by man but how often is it good for an audience to spend an evening in a chain gang? Surely not so often as once a week.

Nothing quite like *I Am a Fugitive* was seen again for many years. Then, in 1938, when the propaganda controversy was at its height, the problem it had raised was presented again by *Boy Slaves*, a picture of peonage in the turpentine camps. Based on a story by a frankly radical writer, Alfred Bein, it was outspoken as few movies have been in the realism of its backgrounds of poverty and its types of Southern officers of the law. An interesting film and an exciting one, it raised again the question of how much horror an audience should be expected to stand.

The next ramification of the propaganda question has an international twist. Some historian of the future may one day be surprised to discover that in the late 1930's the American motion picture industry made a large group of films glorifying every aspect of British virtue from Dr. Barnardo's Homes to the patrolling of the Khyber Pass. *Cavalcade, Lives of a Bengal Lancer, Lord Jeff, Wee Willie Winkie, Susannah of the Mounties, Gunga Din, The Sun Never Sets;* the roll goes on and on. That these films correctly sound the empire note was proved beyond question when King George conferred the Order of the British Empire on C. Aubrey Smith, the English actor to whom Hollywood gives practically permanent employment as a British colonel.

The immediate explanation of this burst of British propaganda is a very simple one. As continental audiences dwindled Britain, which had always stood high, became an even more important section of the American movies' foreign public. It was highly desirable to please Great Britain if possible, and it could be done without sacrifice, for the American public, too, seemed to be stirred with admiration for British empire ideals. Loyalty as the supreme virtue no matter to what you are loyal, courage, hard work, a creed in which *noblesse oblige* is the most intellectual conception; those ideas are easier to grasp and very much easier to dramatize on the screen than social responsibility, the relation of the individual to the state, the necessity for a pacifist to fight tyranny, the nature of democracy, and the similar problems with which the intellectuals want the movies to deal.

The propaganda problem to be decided here is a question of date: In just what period are the eighty-five million American moviegoers living? Is it the middle ages or the twentieth century, the nineteenth century or the world of tomorrow? The intellectuals, living at the uttermost point of the present, consider it one of the functions of art and their artists to point the way to the future. They see no reason why the movies should not march ahead of their audience as the modern American novel at its best is doing. The producers, on the other hand, maintain that it is the function of the motion picture to satisfy its audiences, not to stimulate them, and their guess at the period in which the majority of the eighty-five million are living is about 1854. They do not actually express it, of course, in quite such concrete terms but obviously what they think their public believes in are the social ideals of the British Empire at the time of the Crimean War. The present popularity of the empire pictures might seem to prove their point.

The British glory is magnificent but it looks insignificant beside the great wave of American patriotism which swept the country at about the same time and is still mounting. The chief propaganda question that wave raises is, What is enough of a good thing? How long will American history last at the rate at which the producers are using it up? Is there any chance of the cycle's coming to a close before every era of our past has been steeped in glamour; before each recorded incident of our history from the Revolution to the war of 1917 has served as a background for a love affair; before every national crisis has been settled by one man's loyalty or one woman's charm? Why the producer who would not dream of asking an historical character to wear an anachronous shoebuckle will blithely fit him to the stereotype of romantic drama is another problem of propaganda.

The motion picture epics of America's past are the natural outgrowth of the immortal Western and retain many of its best qualities. They are swift and exciting. They make good use of our spectacular natural backgrounds. They offer the skillful Hollywood research departments opportunity to recreate for us instructive pictures of the lives of our ancestors. But the simplicity of the Western is gone. Into each "epic" the producer seems to feel impelled to pack material enough for ten good movies. All the best stories about a dozen Western scouts are added to the saga of "Wild Bill" Hickok and told in something less than two hours. Or a buffalo stampede, an Indian raid, a stagecoach holdup, a barroom battle, and the building of a railroad are jammed into one film, and the next adds to those a hanging and a prairie fire. The winning of the West pictures are most greedy in their attempts to get in everything but the movies that deal with other historical periods run them often a close second. Enthusiasm for our national past is certainly to be encouraged but should the enthusiasm perhaps have bounds?

Twenty-nine "Americanism" features were announced by the industry as in preparation in January, 1939. Added to these were sixty-three patriotic shorts on subjects ranging from *Remember the Alamo* to *The Bill of Rights*. As its contribution to the World's Fairs Hollywood made *Land of Liberty* compiled from historical films and newsreels taken from the industry's early days right down to the present. And, lest pictures should not be enough, one theater chain after another is commanding the playing at each performance of "The Star Spangled Banner."

One of the "Americanism" features, *Confessions of a Nazi Spy*, raised in the spring of 1939 what is perhaps the most curious propaganda problem of all. The story was based on a Federal investigation which had been filling the metropolitan papers. The facts were dramatized, the people became individuals, but there was no love interest at all, almost no personal plot. The method of telling the story was adapted from the technique of *The March of Time*. The direction was rapid and very skillful; the acting excellent. The story did not go beyond the facts but it was enormously exciting. The film was in fine so bitter and convincing a denouncement of *Bund* activities in the United States that a great many people looked at it in alarm. Was this perhaps going too far, unleashing too suddenly the powers of propaganda? Was there not danger that such a film would stir the same illogical national hatreds that darkened the country in 1917 and '18? *Confessions of a Nazi Spy* went out across the country and it immediately became apparent that the intellectuals were disturbed about the wrong thing. The audiences in the smaller towns and cities had followed the spy case only casually in the newspapers. They were interested in the film—it did well at the box-office—but they were not particularly excited about it. A good picture, they said, but of course all that spy stuff is not true; it's just a movie. Here, posed sharply for the first time, was a strangely difficult problem of propaganda.

But *Confessions of a Nazi Spy* answered a question as well as posing one. It demonstrated that first-class actors and directors were eager to work with really significant material. The aesthetic saviors of the movies and the social saviors might attain their ends by the same road. Francis Lederer, who was cast as the chief Nazi agent, was a Czecho-

The screen is telling Americans about America. Our natural scenery is utilized for spectacular backgrounds: "Dodge City." National heroes are brought to life: Henry Fonda as "Young Mr. Lincoln."

"Juarez," which dramatizes the principles of democracy, is proving that the millions have no objection to films with ideas.

Slovakian who accepted the role and played it with all his power as a piece of patriotic service. Edward G. Robinson, who had been trying to persuade his studio to let him make *Professor Mamlock*, got some compensation out of the role of the G-man who breaks the German spy ring. And two other films which appeared at about the same time strengthened the point. Henry Fonda played *Young Mr. Lincoln* with a dedicated sincerity which was touching as well as convincing. Paul Muni, who has more choice in the matter of parts than most actors, was interested in the difficult task of embodying *Juarez*, the Indian who became President of the Mexican Republic.

Both these Hollywood films very nearly succeeded in satisfying the intellectuals. The dramatization of its heroes is undoubtedly one of the effective ways of unifying a nation's ideals. The legend of the youth of the great democratic hero was beautifully accurate in spirit if not in fact. John Ford, director of *Young Mr. Lincoln*, recreated with marked success the Illinois town of a century ago and used his special skill with half lights and shadows, the flicker of election-parade torches, the play of sunlight through branches on the river, to intensify the sense of veiled greatness which was a striking characteristic of Fonda's Lincoln. *Juarez*, too, glorified a democratic hero and its very title was significant of a new order. Ten years ago, as John Mosher pointed out in the *New*

Yorker, it would have been called "Maximilian
and Carlotta" or just "Carlotta." In 1939 it was
good business to put the emphasis on the power
of democracy and the unimportance of race. Long,
elaborate, and impressive *Juarez* disturbed some of
the intellectuals by its variance from accepted rules
of technique. Slow paced even in its most exciting
scenes it depended for many of its emotional
effects upon the extraordinary beauty of its lighting and camera work or the eloquent diction of its
actors, Muni, Brian Aherne, Bette Davis. Having
agreed on the axiom that a moving picture must
move, and preferably move fast, some of the intellectuals at first thought *Juarez* dull. They were
annoyed by its sometimes overwritten dialogue,
its, for them, too obvious points about democracy,
but another lesson in propaganda was at least suggested when the eighty-five million flocked to see
it and its box-office score mounted steadily.

The intellectuals may seem to be coming into
their own but their problems are not yet at an end.
Are these fine films portents, they inquire, or are
they merely isolated phenomena? They represent,
after all, the initiative of only a few companies.
Add to the pictures already mentioned Charlie
Chaplin's satire *The Dictator*, now in preparation,
and Warner Brothers' announcement of *The
Bishop Who Walked with God*, the story of Pas-
tor Niemoller; what else have you to look forward
to? Paramount's *Our Leading Citizen* is definitely

antilabor. Metro and Walter Wanger alternately announce and withdraw Sinclair Lewis's *It Can't Happen Here* and Vincent Sheean's *Personal History*. Gossip has it that a bank instructed Zanuck to buy Steinbeck's *The Grapes of Wrath* in order to keep it from being filmed. There are other rumors of the same hue. Certainly the industry's welcome to ideas on the screen is no more than half-hearted. The general attitude seems to be not that the movies are at last a mature art but that this desire for films with content is one of those unaccountable public whims which will fade out eventually like the craze for spectacular musicals or the enthusiasm for Marlene Dietrich.

The intellectuals, on their side, are discovering that getting ideas into the movies is not the simple matter of yes and no it looked while they were fighting the doctrine of pure entertainment. They must decide, they find, whether wanting ideas on the screen means wanting also ideas of which you passionately disapprove. They must decide how far, when it becomes essential to show the dark side of life, it is possible to go without debasing your audience or driving them away. They must discover how the eighty-five million, accustomed to discounting the magnificent exaggerations of Hollywood, can be made to believe the truth when they meet it. We have supposed that, given the opportunity, the American film could say whatever it wanted to say. We are beginning to see that there are in the movies two essential techniques: the technique of handling apparatus, in which the American makers of films are almost supreme masters; and the technique of handling ideas which they have just begun to learn.

INDEX